THE LAW OF CONFESSION

*Revolutionize Your Life and Rewrite Your Future
With the Power of Words*

Dr. Bill Winston

Harrison House
Tulsa, Oklahoma

Unless otherwise noted, all scripture quotations are taken from the *King James Version* of the Bible.

Scripture quotations marked AMP are taken from the *Amplified® Bible.* Copyright © 1954, 1958, 1962, 1964, 1965, 1987 by The Lockman Foundation. Used by permission. (www.Lockman.org)

Verses marked TLB are taken from *The Living Bible* © 1971. Used by permission of Tyndale House Publishers, Inc., Wheaton, Illinois 60189. All rights reserved.

13 12 11 10   10 9 8 7 6 5 4 3

The Law of Confession:
Revolutionize Your Life and Rewrite Your Future With the Power of Words
ISBN 13: 978-1-57794-969-5
ISBN 10: 1-57794-969-2
Copyright © 2009 Dr. Bill Winston
Bill Winston Ministries
P.O. Box 947
Oak Park, Illinois 60303-0947
www.bwm.org

Published by Harrison House Publishers
P. O. Box 35035
Tulsa, Oklahoma 74153
www.harrisonhouse.com

TABLE OF CONTENTS

Introduction

What is the basic definition of a law? *Noah Webster's 1828 Dictionary* defines a law as "that which is laid, set, or fixed."[1] Another definition I like is that a law is a principle based on the predictable consequences of an act. For example, physical laws tell you that if you throw a ball up in the air, it will fall back to the ground. There is only one way the ball will always fall once thrown up and that is down. A certain act will yield a certain result.

Another definition Noah Webster gives for a law is, "a rule, particularly an established or a permanent rule prescribed by the supreme power of a state to its subjects for regulating their actions, particularly their social actions."[2] In simplest terms, a law has the power to govern. Governments pass laws that lay down, set, or fix what is legal and what is illegal. The laws of a natural government can change as society and culture change. However, in the kingdom, God's laws, spiritual and natural, cannot be changed.

Let's look at a natural law: the law of gravity. As a little child, we found out quickly what happens when we lose our balance or our footing. The law of gravity brought us right down on a part of our body God padded especially for that! As we grew up, our respect and understanding for the law of gravity grew, and eventually we learned how to work it to our advantage and to stay safe.

Sir Isaac Newton discovered the law of gravity which basically says that if you drop something, it will always go down; it will never go up. This law also says if you drop something of a given weight from a certain height, like from the top of a three-story building, it will reach the ground in a certain length of time, no matter who you are and no matter where on this Earth you are when you drop it.

The Bible tells us that everything we observe in creation speaks of our Creator.

> Because that which may be known of God is manifest in them; for God hath shewed it unto them.
>
> For the invisible things of him from the creation of the world are clearly seen, being understood by the things that are made, even his eternal power and Godhead; so that they are without excuse.
>
> Romans 1:19-20

All laws created by God reflect His character and nature. When we explore the natural world, we can't help but see our Creator in His creation. For example, the law of gravity—just like God—is no respecter of persons (Acts 10:34). It works for everyone: male or female, black or white, rich or poor, saved or unsaved.

I had to learn several physical laws when I joined the Air Force and became a pilot. As a new recruit, they sent me to ground school. It was called ground school because it taught us all about flying on the ground, before we actually flew in the air. There was a good reason for that. By the time we got up in the air with our flight instructor, we needed to know what was causing us to fly—and what could cause us to crash! The purpose of ground school was to prepare us to fly *successfully.*

In ground school they taught us there are four basic laws that govern flying—the law of thrust, the law of gravity, the law of lift, and the law of drag. Thrust takes you forward, gravity pulls you down, lift draws you up, and drag holds you back. Then they began teaching us how an airplane operates within these laws so it can take off, fly, and land.

Engineers have discovered how these laws work so they can use this knowledge to design all different types of airplanes for all kinds of purposes. They know exactly how each plane is going to fly and what it is capable of doing. What's interesting is that these physical or natural laws existed in the Garden of Eden, but it took mankind until the beginning of the twentieth century to figure out how these four laws would work together to benefit mankind in what we know today as air travel.

When we first got to ground school, most of us were still ignorant of these four laws. The instructors would take us up in a little, single-engine Cessna 172 propeller plane. They would do some stunts to shake us up a bit, and some of the guys would get sick. The instructors made sure each of us had a bag with us! Young recruits got sick mostly because of fear. However, the more they understood about how the laws worked to make the airplane take off, fly, and land, the less afraid they were.

In flight training we learned these laws on the ground, so that when we got into the air we wouldn't be afraid or anxious. Instead, we would understand how and why we were flying. Now I understand that if I generate enough power in the plane to reach a certain speed on the runway, that airplane will lift off every time. It doesn't matter if it is a Boeing 747 jumbo or just a little single engine Piper Cub. But people who don't understand those laws can board one of those big birds and bite their nails the entire time because they have no understanding of the laws that govern them at that moment. To them, it's a mystery.

This is why God tells us in the Bible,

Get wisdom, get understanding: forget it not; neither decline from the words of my mouth. Forsake her not, and she shall preserve thee: love her, and she shall keep thee. Wisdom is the principal thing; therefore get wisdom: and with all thy getting get understanding. Exalt her, and she shall promote thee: she shall bring thee to honour, when thou dost embrace her.

Proverbs 4:5-8

In this book we are going to get wisdom and understanding about another law: the law of confession. The law of confession is one of the basic, fundamental laws that govern this universe and determine our destiny. We are going to study it and discover timeless truths that will give us understanding and take all the fear out of our hearts, so that we will walk in a display of wisdom and power that we never imagined possible.

Because many people have no revelation of the power of their words, they have caused themselves undo hardship. Many people failed when things became difficult, only because they lost their confession. The Bible plainly teaches that, "Death and life are in the power of the tongue" (Proverbs 18:21). In other words, your words reflect your fate, not the devil, not your nation or background, not your relatives or circumstances.

When you believe and speak words that harmonize with what God has already spoken or declared, you release a force to which everything in the universe has to adjust. The power of the tongue is far beyond anything we can naturally perceive. Thinking positively is always good. It's always better to think positively than to think negatively. It will put you in a better frame of mind, but if that is all you do, it is not going to change anything.

Confession, or speaking in line with God's Word, will change the circumstances in your life. In fact, I'll make a bold statement: There is nothing in the universe so big and so powerful that cannot be turned around with your tongue.

You might say this book is your ground school. You are going to learn how to overcome anything that is pulling you down, supernaturally rise up above it, and discover the complete joy of flying with Jesus by learning how to speak the Word!

Your Words
Have Power

There are different kinds of laws most of us recognize, like the law of gravity we discussed in the introduction. And then we learned about other laws that work with the law of gravity to make an airplane fly: the law of thrust, the law of lift, and the law of drag. These are all natural laws that govern our physical world. However, the Bible reveals to us that there are spiritual laws as well as natural laws.

Spiritual laws govern the spiritual realm, but they also govern physical or natural laws because everything in the natural world came from the spirit world. We know this because the Word says God is a Spirit (John 4:24), and He created everything. He is a Spirit being, who lives in the spirit realm, and He created the entire physical universe—all we encounter in the natural realm—from the spirit realm.

Everything we contact with our physical senses originally came from the heart and mind of a Spirit, God the Creator. Therefore, all things natural or physical are governed by that which is spiritual. The physical laws that govern us in the natural world, then, are a reflection of the spiritual laws that govern over all. Furthermore, just as the law of lift can overcome the law of gravity, spiritual laws can overcome natural laws.

How does this happen? What is the key to making this work? Our words.

The Key to Creation

Through faith we understand that the worlds were framed by the word of God, so that things which are seen were not made of things which do appear.

Hebrews 11:3

The key to all creation [and creativity] is the Word of God. The universe was framed by "the word of God," and this has always been a Word planet. God designed it that way. Hebrews 11:3 describes how God spoke this natural world into being. He used His words (spiritual things that are not seen) to create the physical universe (natural things that are seen). The detailed account of God doing all this is found in Genesis, chapter 1.

And God said, Let there be light: and there was light.
And God said, Let there be a firmament in the midst of the waters, and let it divide the waters from the waters.

And God said, Let the waters under the heaven be gathered together unto one place, and let the dry land appear: and it was so.

And God said, Let the earth bring forth grass, the herb yielding seed, and the fruit tree yielding fruit after his kind, whose seed is in itself, upon the earth: and it was so.

And God said, Let there be lights in the firmament of the heaven to divide the day from the night; and let them be for signs, and for seasons, and for days, and years: And let them be for lights in the firmament of the heaven to give light upon the earth: and it was so.

And God said, Let the waters bring forth abundantly the moving creature that hath life, and fowl that may fly above the earth in the open firmament of heaven.

And God said, Let the earth bring forth the living creature after his kind, cattle, and creeping thing, and beast of the earth after his kind: and it was so.

And God said, Let us make man in our image, after our likeness: and let them have dominion over the fish of the sea, and over the fowl of the air, and over the cattle, and over all the earth, and over every creeping thing that creepeth upon the earth.

Genesis 1:3,6,9,11,14-15,20,24,26 (italics mine)

If you read the entire passage in Genesis 1, after you read, "And God said," you will read, "and it was so." What God says happens! If He said it, you can bank on it.

So shall my word be that goeth forth out of my mouth: it shall not return unto me void, but it shall accomplish that which I please, and it shall prosper in the thing whereto I sent it.

Isaiah 55:11

We could paraphrase that verse as, "It's the Word that does the work."

Another phrase you will read again and again in Genesis 1 is, "and God saw that it was good." God's Word also makes everything good. God is good, and therefore everything He says and creates is good. That's just the way He is, and the Bible tells us in Malachi 3:6 and Hebrews 13:8 that God never changes. Everything He says and does is always good and He always operates and creates the same way: by His Word.

In the New Testament, we read the exact same story of creation.

> In the beginning was the Word, and the Word was with God, and the Word was God.
> The same was in the beginning with God.
> All things were made by him; and without him was not any thing made that was made.
>
> John 1: 1-3

The subject of this passage is the Word. The Word of God made all things! So the key to creation is speaking God's Word.

The Word Planet—Good Or Evil

God created Adam and Eve to operate the same way He operates. As speaking spirits, they were designed to follow His example, using their words to accomplish His plan by being fruitful, multiplying, replenishing, subduing, and

4

taking dominion over the Earth (Genesis 1:26,28). As long as they were in complete unity and one accord with God, life was perfect. Their words reflected God's mind and heart, which meant their lives and everything around them was good. But then the serpent came, tempted Eve, and many things changed.

How did the serpent tempt Eve? He challenged God's Word. He said, "Hath God said…?" (Genesis 3:1). The devil has never changed! He is still trying to cause believers to doubt God's Word today. He knows the power of words, especially God's words.

When Adam and Eve disobeyed God, they left a spiritual existence and fell into a natural one. Their carnal reasoning and physical senses became the extent of their ability. Their spirits were disconnected from God, so their words no longer reflected His heart and mind. After the Fall, their words reflected the sin and death that reigned in their hearts and minds.

These were major changes in their lives—and they weren't good! However, their mandate from God remained the same, and so did the power of their words. Their nature had changed, but they were still to be fruitful, multiply, replenish, subdue, and take dominion. And what they chose to speak out of their mouths would produce either good or evil. Whatever Adam and Eve and their descendants spoke still had the power to determine their destiny and affect the destiny of everything around them; whether they served God or the devil, whether they spoke words of life or words of death.

Finally Jesus came and gave mankind a way back to being spiritually alive to God again. When we receive Him as Lord and Savior, He gives us a new spirit, fills us with His Spirit, and imparts to us the love and nature of God. Now we can commune with God again and speak His Word in faith—but we still have to choose whether to speak life or death.

Words are the most powerful things on this Earth. They can change and rearrange anything—for good or for evil. Jesus explained to His followers how our words produce either good or evil when He said,

> By thy words thou shalt be justified, and by thy words thou shalt be condemned.
>
> Matthew 12:37

Jesus laid it on the line for all of us: What we say matters. Our words will justify us and bring blessing to our lives, or our words will condemn us and bring calamity and sorrow to our lives. Therefore, we need to take heed to what is coming out of our mouths because therein lies our destiny.

We know God has a plan for our lives, a plan that is good and full of peace (Jeremiah 29:11). We will either talk our way into it or talk our way out of it.

The Law of Agreement

The law of confession becomes even more powerful when we also function according to God's law of agreement. Jesus taught about this law.

Again I say unto you, That if two of you shall agree on earth as touching any thing that they shall ask, it shall be done for them of my Father which is in heaven.

Matthew 18:19

Speaking in agreement with God and each other has always been God's plan, but sinful man has used these laws for evil instead of good. For example, Noah and his family were the only ones of their time who still worshipped and served God, so God preserved them when He sent the flood to cleanse the Earth of all the evil. However, it wasn't long before Noah's descendants also began to ignore God's desires and "do their own thing." The Bible tells us that words were a major part of the problem.

Instead of obeying God and spreading out over all the Earth to replenish it and bring His presence, Noah's descendants rebelled against God, stayed together, and settled down in the plain of Shinar. They began to build the city of Babel, which later became Babylon, a location that has caused problems for God's people ever since. Under their leader, Nimrod, the people at Babel began constructing a tower, which they planned to build higher and higher until it went right into Heaven. (See Genesis 10:8-10, 11:1-5.)

Now we know there is only one way to Heaven, and it isn't by our good works, no matter how high they reach toward Heaven. We can't build or work our way into God's good graces. The only way to Heaven is through the shed blood and resurrection life of Jesus Christ. But these people had become so wicked they had developed their own religion, a demonic religion that was in complete defiance of God and His way of salvation.

The people of Babylon had one thing going for them, however: They were in total agreement with one another. The problem was, they were out of agreement with God! They were deceived into thinking they could save themselves by building this tower right into Heaven, but then something happened that put a halt to the whole operation. The tower and the city surrounding it were never finished.

What stopped Nimrod and the people from completing their tower and the city that surrounded it? After all, they were unified and motivated. Genesis 11:6-8 says the Lord saw what they were doing and said,

> Behold, the people is one, and they have all one language; and this they begin to do: and now nothing will be restrained from them, which they have imagined to do. Go to, let us go down, and there confound their language, that they may not understand one another's speech. So the LORD scattered them abroad from thence upon the face of all the earth: and they left off to build the city.

The tower and the city surrounding it were never completed because God "confounded their language." He caused different people groups to speak different languages, so they couldn't understand one another. This is why the tower is called the Tower of Babel. Suddenly there was utter confusion. The people were no longer in agreement because their means of communication had been cut off. Thus, they stopped building and scattered all over the

Earth, each people group or tribe going off by themselves to form their own nation.

God stopped them by doing something with their *words*. He said as long as they were of one language—which allowed them to be in agreement—they could accomplish anything. God had to intervene before they destroyed themselves completely, and He did that by changing the words they spoke.

The lesson learned from the Tower of Babel is that the words you speak are powerful, but they are even more powerful when you and someone else are speaking in complete agreement. You can see that the words you speak have the ability to bring unity or disharmony, blessing or cursing, life or death. They can cause you to stay in one place or move to another place. But in agreement with others, words can accomplish whatever you can imagine.

God's will for your words is first to agree with His Word. Then He wants you to agree with someone else according to His Word. He wants you to do this so He can bless you in every way imaginable. Consider what the people of Babylon could have accomplished had they been in total agreement with God as well as each other. They could have done anything they imagined, and every bit of it would have glorified God. That is His dream for the body of Christ.

The Element of Time

Studying the law of confession also brings us into a new understanding of time. We are to be like God, and He lives outside of time. He knows the end from the beginning.

That's why Jesus said, "Your Father knoweth what things ye have need of, before ye ask him" (Matthew 6:8). When we pray and speak His Word over our problem, we have more confidence knowing He knew what we needed before we even knew we had a problem!

> Blessed be the God and Father of our Lord Jesus Christ, who hath blessed us with all spiritual blessings in heavenly places in Christ:
>
> According as he hath chosen us in him *before the foundation of the world,* that we should be holy and without blame before him in love.
>
> Ephesians 1:3-4 (italics mine)

God didn't say He was going to bless you. He said, "hath blessed." In verse 4 He said that He knew you would accept Jesus as your Lord and Savior and become His child before He created the universe. As we go through life, we must remember that God doesn't start until He's finished. Whatever He is calling us to do, He had it all worked it out before the Earth or people existed.

> For we are his workmanship, created in Christ Jesus unto good works, which God hath before ordained that we should walk in them.
>
> Ephesians 2:10

The gifts and callings we walk in today were ordained by God long before we were even born. All we have to do is agree with Him and walk in them. Biblical confession means we agree with God by saying what He has said, knowing He already settled this thing before the foundation of the world. For example, if you say you don't have peace, you have just disagreed with Ephesians 1:3. You are not saying what God says about you. He says you have all spiritual blessings, which includes peace. You have peace now.

What you should have done if you felt a lack of peace was to declare, "I have peace with God through Jesus Christ" (Romans 5:1). When you speak the Word of God you are declaring what is already real and present in your spirit, and your faith confession is bringing that peace into your soul. Everything you will ever need for your life on Earth is already yours in Heaven. And what brings it from Heaven to Earth? Your confession of faith in God and His Word.

The world has programmed you to say things based on what you see, but you are to say things based on what God said in His Word, not what you see. When you speak from your spirit according to the Word of God, you will bring what you need from the spirit realm into the natural realm. This is how Jesus operated. He functioned in the spirit realm and the natural realm at the same time, and He spoke in complete harmony with both realms.

Jesus knew that the spirit ruled the natural, and the spiritual realm is outside of time. This is why He could heal the sick even before He was scourged and went to the Cross. He had been slain before the foundation of the world (Revelation 13:8). In the spirit realm, it was already done. There is no time in the spirit; therefore God can override time, and so can you and I.

When I was holding a meeting in Virginia a lady came to the altar with a fracture in her arm that had happened three days before. I said, "Alright, let me show you how the kingdom of God works. In the kingdom there is no time, and I'm a representative of the kingdom." I laid my hand on her arm and said, "In the name of Jesus, be healed." She started moving her arm and then began crying. It was totally healed in seconds. Not two or three weeks or months or years. Why? I used the spiritual law of confession and God accelerated the natural healing time.

You have been designed to use the law of confession to override time. You can pray for your great-great grandchildren, whom you will never live to see and who will never hear your prayers, and your prayers will be answered. Some of us are saved because of what our grandmamma believed and spoke. The Word works beyond the grave!

Your Purpose

You are to operate like Jesus operates. You are not subject to the things people are subject to who don't know Jesus, who are not born again. They live only by their physical senses and carnal reasoning, but you are to live like Jesus: in two realms. You live in the natural realm according to the truth that is in the spiritual realm. You live in the knowledge of eternal life and God's eternal Word. You do this by using your words, which are life-changing and world-impacting.

God's desire is to bring you into your wealthy place that He has prepared for you (Psalm 66:12), and He has established that no one can stop you from reaching your wealthy place but you. Stop and think about that. No man, no principality or power, no government, no class or system, no racial prejudice—nothing or no one can stop you from coming in to the wealthy place God has prepared for you but you! That's just what God said to Joshua.

> There shall not any man be able to stand before thee all the days of thy life: as I was with Moses, so I will be with thee: I will not fail thee, nor forsake thee.
>
> Joshua 1:5

When God is with you and you are speaking words in full agreement with His will and His Word, no person or power can stop His will from coming to pass in your life. And He is with you! He promised never to leave you or forsake you (Hebrews 13:5)—and you know He means what He says.

You need to have complete understanding that the life you create for yourself is the one you speak out, either God's will in faith or something else in faith. Much of what happens in your life starts with the words you speak. If you don't like where you are now, you will waste your time blaming God, other people, or the weather. If you want your life to change, then you must change the words you speak. When your words are right in line with God's Word, your life will be transformed in a supernatural way.

You are never going to see anything in your life that hasn't come out of your mouth. Somebody asked me, "Well, what happens if you can't speak?" We know God looks on the heart and will give those who cannot speak some way of expressing their confession of faith. How do we know? Because God is love, and He is full of grace and mercy.

For those of us who can speak, we must learn about the law of confession and operate in it. We can have what we say! That is the power of our words.

2

The Confession That Brings Success

We saw how the law of gravity governs our movement in the natural realm. Now we will discover how the law of confession governs our lives from the spiritual realm. Words have spiritual power, and they are not to be taken lightly. Jesus said it like this,

> The words that I speak unto you, they are spirit, and they are life.
>
> John 6:63

Most people have not made the connection between what they say and what they have in life. They have no idea the two are connected. And many Christians really don't understand that their words are spiritual and powerful, especially when they are speaking God's Word.

There are also a lot of different ideas in the church about what confession is. One idea of confession a lot of people relate to is when someone confesses to a crime. Criminals are convicted in courts of law because they sign a full "confession" to committing a crime. Another common meaning for confession is most widely known from the Roman Catholic religion. You may have heard a Catholic friend say, "I'm going to confession," which means, "I'm going to confess to the priest a sin I committed."

Both of these examples of confession have a negative connotation, and traditionally we tend to think of confession in a somewhat negative way. Many churches preach and teach the confession of our sins, weaknesses, and faults—and there is a rightful place for that. The television is full of shows about criminals confessing their crimes, and we are glad when that happens. But we are programmed from childhood to believe that confession only involves sin and crime, so we think of confession as a negative thing.

There are really four types of biblical confession. The first is the confession John the Baptist gave to the Jews when they came to be water baptized by him.

> John did baptize in the wilderness, and preach the baptism of repentance for the remission of sins.
>
> Mark 1:4

This confession is the confession of sin, an acknowledgement that we are sinners in need of a savior.

The second confession is the typical confession of a sinner acknowledging the lordship of Jesus Christ.

That if thou shalt confess with thy mouth the Lord Jesus,
and shalt believe in thine heart that God hath raised Him
from the dead, thou shalt be saved.

Romans 10:9

The sinner doesn't confess all their sins when they get
saved. They simply confess Jesus Christ as their Lord. Once
a person confesses that Jesus is their Lord, the Bible says
they become a "new creature" (2 Corinthians 5:17). With
this confession all their sins are forgiven, their spirit is
regenerated, and they become a child of God and a member
of the body of Christ. This is the most important confession
that any person will make in their lifetime. Not only does it
change their eternal destiny, but it also changes the very
essence of who they are. They become a righteous child of
God and receive His nature.

The third confession is made by believers when they find
themselves out of fellowship with the Lord because they
have disobeyed the Word or the Spirit. It is the believer's
confession of sin that's spelled out in 1 John 1:9.

If we confess our sins, he is faithful and just to forgive us
our sins, and to cleanse us from all unrighteousness.

This is what we are to do when we miss the mark, and we
all miss it sometime! The good news is that, as children of
God, forgiveness and cleansing are always available to us.
The Bible also says that when we confess our sins, God not
only forgives us but also *forgets* our sins.

As far as the east is from the west, so far hath He removed
our transgressions from us.

Psalms 103:12

For I will forgive their iniquity, and I will remember their sin no more.

Jeremiah 31:34

This third confession allows us to walk with God the way Adam and Eve walked with Him before the Fall. Our sin can never separate us from God again because the blood of Jesus continually cleanses us from *all* unrighteousness. As Romans 5:1 says, we have peace with God through Jesus Christ.

Finally, the fourth type of confession is the one most Christians don't know—the one Satan doesn't want them to know because it brings our divine destiny to pass and impacts the world around us with the love and truth and glory of God. The fourth confession is speaking God's will and Word in faith.

Homologeo: Saying What God Says

God created Adam and Eve in His image and after His likeness (Genesis 1:26), which meant He intended for them to operate just the way He does and God has never said anything that He didn't want to come to pass. When God speaks something it is so.

God is not a man, that he should lie; neither the son of man, that he should repent: hath he said, and shall he not do it? or hath he spoken, and shall he not make it good?

Numbers 23:19

God doesn't lie—ever. He has no reason to repent because He has never sinned and never will sin. Sin is not in Him. This description of our God points to one thing: when it comes to His Word, He always speaks the truth and what He says goes. If He has said it, it is going to happen. We can have complete trust in Him and His Word.

The Greek word translated "confession" in the New Testament is *homologeo,* and it denotes this fourth kind of confession. It is a compound word: *homo,* which means "the same," and *logeo,* which means "word."[1] A more specific definition is: "to say the same thing as another, i.e. to agree with, assent; to concede;... to profess; to declare openly."[2]

What *homologeo* means for the Christian believer is to say the same thing that God says, to agree with, assent, concede to, profess, and declare openly what God says in His Word. That is what you and I were created to do. It makes no difference what the circumstances or situation might look like in the natural, we have to look past the trouble we may be experiencing in our health, our finances, our relationships, or our soul, and say what God says. That always should be our confession.

You aren't supposed to be looking for a path you can follow. You are simply to walk in the path God has already laid out for you, and you begin that journey with your words. It is a path of blessing if you are speaking what He says about you and what He wants for you. *Homologeo* (saying what God says) is the type of confession that gets you on the way to obtaining the promises God has given to you in His Word.

The law of confession—and especially this fourth kind of confession, *homologeo,* or speaking what God says— has been a mystery to the modern believer. It is right there in the Bible, but you have to dig for it. Satan will do everything he can to keep you from finding this law and walking in it because the more revelation you get about the law of confession, the more dangerous you are to him and the kingdom of darkness.

The Church needs to be taught the power of saying the same thing God says. We need to see and understand the creative ability He has given us as we agree with, assent to, concede to, profess, and declare openly the Word and the will of the Lord. This is how we will possess the inheritance Jesus died to give us—to fulfill our highest callings and to be conformed to the image of Christ Jesus.

Where Your Words Go

Wherefore, holy brethren, partakers of the heavenly calling, consider the Apostle and High Priest of our profession, Christ Jesus.

Hebrews 3:1

When you speak God's Word there are things that go into motion that you can't see with the natural eye. This verse reveals where your words go and how they work in the spirit realm. "Holy brethren" is you, and you are a partaker of the "heavenly calling." What is that calling? To speak the Word and will of God into the Earth. And how do you do that? You are to consider (think about, ponder, and meditate on) Jesus.

Jesus is first your Apostle, the one who was sent by God to save you. He is the High Priest of your profession. Guess what Greek word is translated "profession"? *Homologia,* which is the feminine form of *homologeo!* Of course, it means "to agree, confess, say the same."[3] Your profession or confession of faith goes right to Jesus, your High Priest, when you say what God and His Word say.

In the Old Testament, once a year the high priest went into the Holy of Holies to make a sacrifice on behalf of all the children of Israel for all the sins they had committed that year. He was doing something before God for everybody. Jesus became our eternal sacrifice and High Priest when He carried His own blood into the Holy of Holies in Heaven to atone for all the sins of mankind for all time. Now, He is the High Priest of our confession of faith. That means our words go right to Him in Heaven.

Our words are not the only words Jesus hears in Heaven, however.

The Heavenly Court

And the great dragon was cast out, that old serpent, called the Devil, and Satan, which deceiveth the whole world: he was cast out into the earth, and his angels were cast out with him.

And I heard a loud voice saying in heaven, Now is come salvation, and strength, and the kingdom of our God, and the power of his Christ: for the accuser of our brethren is cast down, which accused them before our God day and night.

And they overcame him by the blood of the Lamb, and by the word of their testimony; and they loved not their lives unto the death.

Revelation 12:9-11

Satan is making accusations against you to God day and night. His words condemn and put you down, but Jesus hears your confessions, whether you are repenting of your sins according to 1 John 1:9 or speaking life to a dead situation. You overcome Satan and his accusations by the blood of the Lamb and the word of your testimony—declaring the Word of God.

"They loved not their lives unto the death" does not mean you will die when you make your confession to Jesus. It means, like Shadrach, Meshach, and Abednego, you have no concern about your life even in the face of death because your life is already eternally sealed in Jesus Christ. Like those three Hebrew boys, you can say in the face of any danger, "The God that I serve will deliver us!" (see Daniel 3:17), and your words will go straight into Heaven and take the devil down.

> But ye are come unto mount Sion, and unto the city of the living God, the heavenly Jerusalem, and to an innumerable company of angels,
>
> To the general assembly and church of the firstborn, which are written in heaven, and to God the Judge of all, and to the spirits of just men made perfect,
>
> And to Jesus the mediator of the new covenant, and to the blood of sprinkling, that speaketh better things than that of Abel.

Hebrews 12:22-24

God is the righteous Judge and Jesus is the one who enforces our New Covenant with Him. Jesus is also our attorney. When Satan accuses us, Jesus is the one who defends us in the heavenly court.

> My little children, these things write I unto you, that ye sin not. And if any man sin, we have an advocate with the Father, Jesus Christ the righteous.
>
> 1 John 2:1

"Advocate" is another word for attorney. You've got the best lawyer in the universe! If you have any doubt that He is for you, just look at the Cross. He is for you so much that He died for you.

When the devil makes his case, the Judge turns to Jesus and says, "I want to hear from the defense now."

Jesus says, "I call My blood to the stand to testify."

You remember when Cain slew Abel, God told Cain that his brother's blood was crying to Him from the ground (Genesis 4:10). Blood speaks! Hebrews 12:24 says that the blood of Jesus speaks better things than Abel's blood. Abel's blood called for justice, but Jesus' blood fulfilled all the requirements of divine justice. That's why just before He died Jesus said, "It is finished" (John 19:30).

The blood of Jesus takes the stand and testifies that you are forgiven and cleansed. You have been made righteous and are innocent because His blood paid the price for your sin. The blood of the Lamb speaks loudly and clearly that God's justice has been served where your sins are concerned—but the Judge is not yet satisfied.

The testimony of the blood of the Lamb alone is not going to settle it with the Judge because in the Book He wrote, "that in the mouth of two or three witnesses every word may be established" (Matthew 18:16). Jesus has the witness of His blood, but He needs another witness—you. This is why Revelation 12:11 says you overcome by the blood of the Lamb *and* the word of your testimony.

> For by thy words thou shalt be justified, and by thy words thou shalt be condemned.
>
> Matthew 12:37

Condemned means put in bondage and imprisoned. That's what happens to you when you do not testify and speak what God speaks about you, about your situation, or anything that concerns you. Whether you need forgiveness or healing or a financial breakthrough—you must testify. You are justified by the blood of the Lamb and your testimony of the Word of God.

You must say what God says in His Word. What you feel, what your neighbor said, or what your philosophy teacher taught you will not please the Judge. He cannot hear those words! He can only hear His Word spoken in faith. Only the word of your testimony will justify you.

In the heavenly court, after the blood of Jesus cries out "not guilty" and "healed" and "righteous," then your testimony of God's Word reaches the Judge's ears and you are justified. When you are justified by God you are acquitted and freed of all sin and able to prosper in every area of life. Thank God for the blood! Thank God for the Word! And thank God for the law of confession that brings the reality of our justification and freedom into our natural lives.

The Way to Fight

You must remember that God is positive and proactive, and He loves it when you are too. When you are in a battle, He doesn't mind if you cast your cares on Him and release all the negative stuff that is bottled up in your heart. But remember, He already knows what's bothering you; and once you have bared your soul to Him, you must listen to the Holy Spirit's instructions. You will never get anywhere being negative and continuing to confess the problem; you must become focused on Him and hear the answer.

The Holy Spirit always has the answer and the answer is either right out of God's Word or it completely lines up with God's Word. The Holy Spirit's answer will come from within your spirit and maintain peace inside. His answer is your confession from that moment on. Confessing the word He gives you will solve your problem and win your battle. If there is anything in your life that needs turning around, saying what God says about it will turn it around.

It helps if you have someone standing with you, someone close who will hold you accountable for what you speak. You need somebody in your life who will take you to task when you say something God didn't say, someone who is not afraid to look you in the eye and ask, "What are you saying? Do you really mean that? Is that what you want?"

When my wife and I first learned about the law of confession and I began to teach it to our congregation, we both began to practice it. We agreed to keep each other accountable. If I slipped and said something that went crosswise to the Word of God, something my wife knew I didn't really want to come to pass, she would say, "Well Sweetheart, if that's what you want, I agree with you."

That would catch me up quick! I'd say, "Wait a minute. Are you going to use my own teaching on me?" I couldn't get mad at her. I thanked God for her! She was exhorting me and encouraging me to stay on the right road, the road to my wealthy place in God.

One of the best things that ever happened to me, my family, and my church, was the revelation of the law of confession, and specifically, the fourth kind of confession: *homologeo,* or saying what God says. In our individual lives and corporately, we came into agreement with God's Word and with one another. We began to declare His will and Word over our lives, knowing our words were going straight to Jesus in Heaven, defeating every scheme and accusation of the enemy, and releasing the power of God into every situation. We learned that the moment we win the battle over our words, we win the battle!

Satan's Lies About Your Words

Satan went after Adam and Eve and the whole human race because he knew God had given us authority in the Earth. And how did we express and use that authority? With our words! So Satan put us under his thumb by destroying our understanding of the power and value of our words. He convinced us that our words didn't matter. As a result, we stopped believing that anything we said would come to pass or have any consequences. He convinced us that words weren't spirit. They weren't life. Words were just empty speech.

Do you remember the old song we sang as kids: "Sticks and stones may break my bones but words will never hurt me"? That was right out of the enemy's playbook! This is a lie because words can and do hurt us. We have all been offended and wounded by words spoken to us in anger, jealousy, fear, or hatred. Apart from knowing Jesus and the power of forgiveness in the Christian life, many people never get over some of the terrible words that have been spoken to them.

Satan's grand deception is that our words are powerless and ineffectual. When we believe that lie, we believe our words have nothing to do with the way our lives go. Of course, this was never what God wanted for us. His desire has always been that our words establish exactly who we are, where we go, and what we have in life—and all for our good. When Jesus came to restore us to the Father, He had a lot to say about what we say. He made it clear that our words have power and value.

Words Are Spirit

Jesus said His words are spirit and full of abundant life, that His words have spiritual power to overcome any natural challenge.

> It is the spirit that quickeneth; the flesh profiteth nothing: the words that I speak unto you, they are spirit, and they are life.
>
> John 6:63

We know spiritual laws govern natural laws, so it follows that spiritual words have dominion over natural words or natural things. Through the law of confession, God teaches us how to operate in spiritual law and have dominion over natural things. This is what God commanded us to do when He created us.

> And God blessed them, and God said unto them, Be fruitful, and multiply, and replenish the earth, and subdue it: and have dominion over the fish of the sea, and over the fowl of the air, and over every living thing that moveth upon the earth.
>
> Genesis 1:28

Our purpose is to be fruitful, multiply, replenish the Earth, subdue it, and have dominion or rule over every living thing on the Earth. We are the caretakers and stewards of God's creation. How are we to do that? By our words.

In Hebrews 1:3, it says that God holds creation together by "the word of His power." It is His spoken Word that holds this universe together. Even science is beginning to realize this truth. In Genesis 1:3 God said, "Let there be light: and there was light." Today scientists tell us that the universe is still expanding at the speed of light. Why is this happening? The Bible says God spoke light into being, and His words are Spirit and life—eternal life. Once God says something and puts it in motion, nothing can stop it.

Since God spoke the universe into being, it's going to stay right where it is because that was His Word. You're not going to wake up one morning and find the sun coming up in the West. Everything will function the way He said it would because His Word is holding it in place.

Because God has made us in His own image, the words we speak are much more than mere sound. Sound is what you hear with your natural ears, but your words are spirit and life to your heart. As a believer, you have probably experienced those times when someone was preaching or teaching the Word, and something they said pierced your heart and went deep inside you. Those words are still alive in you. You keep hearing those words resonate in your whole being because they are spirit and they are living. They bring life with them when they are deposited in your heart.

When you became a new creature in Christ, the old thinking about your words not having any power passed away. Think about it: It was the words you spoke, declaring Jesus as your Lord and Savior, which brought you out of the kingdom of darkness into the kingdom of God! Now you are God's child, and your eyes are being opened to the truth that your words are spirit, and they have power if you believe what you say.

Believing and Speaking

Most of us know the following story of the fig tree. Jesus used it to illustrate the power of words spoken in faith.

> And Jesus entered into Jerusalem, and into the temple: and when he had looked round about upon all things, and now the eventide was come, he went out unto Bethany with the twelve.
>
> And on the morrow, when they were come from Bethany, he was hungry:
>
> And seeing a fig tree afar off having leaves, he came, if haply he might find any thing thereon: and when he came

to it, he found nothing but leaves; for the time of figs was not yet.

And Jesus answered and said unto it, No man eat fruit of thee hereafter for ever. And his disciples heard it.

Mark 11:11-14

The disciples heard Jesus talk to a tree! Our Lord and Savior actually spoke to a material thing that had no ears or mouth or way of communicating. They were getting used to this, however, because in Mark 4:39 Jesus had "rebuked the wind, and said unto the sea, Peace, be still. And the wind ceased, and there was a great calm." They saw that when Jesus spoke to the natural world, it obeyed Him.

After Jesus cursed the fig tree, He didn't go back to check on that tree every five minutes to see if His words had worked. When He spoke the words, He knew the tree was as good as gone. He believed everything He said would come to pass. However, Peter hadn't taken hold of the law of confession yet, so he was astonished when they passed by the fig tree on their way out of town and saw what had happened to it.

And in the morning, as they passed by, they saw the fig tree dried up from the roots.

And Peter calling to remembrance saith unto him, Master, behold, the fig tree which thou cursedst is withered away.

And Jesus answering saith unto them, Have faith in God.

For verily I say unto you, That whosoever shall say unto this mountain, Be thou removed, and be thou cast into the sea; and shall not doubt in his heart, but shall believe that

31

those things which he saith shall come to pass; he shall have whatsoever he saith.

Therefore I say unto you, What things soever ye desire, when ye pray, believe that ye receive them, and ye shall have them.

Mark 11:20-24

The first thing Jesus said was, "Have faith in God." Whenever we are praying and declaring the Word of God with our mouths, we need to have faith in Him to perform His Word. If we don't believe He will do what He says He will do, then we confess it in vain. Nothing will happen.

Now I want to give you a little practical instruction here. If you are having a hard time believing the Word you are praying and wanting to believe, just keep confessing it and meditating on it until it becomes more real to you than the problem you are facing. Romans 10:17 says that faith comes by hearing by the Word of God, so if you just keep hearing the truth, faith will rise up and the Word will be established in your heart.

Jesus demonstrated the predictable consequences of speaking words of faith. He would have been astonished if the fig tree had *not* been dried up when they came back the next day! That's the kind of faith in our words we have to develop. We have to believe that after we have spoken God's will and Word over a situation, we can walk away and rest in the knowledge that the words we spoke carried the power of God, and what we said must come to pass.

It is absolutely vital that you make the connection between what you say with your mouth and what happens in your life, but that connection will be fruitless if you don't believe what you are saying. Remember, Satan's big deception is that your words have no power or value. He does not want you to believe anything you say, especially when you are speaking God's Word over a situation.

Vain Words

Let no man deceive you with vain words: for because of these things cometh the wrath of God upon the children of disobedience.

Ephesians 5:6

We must increase the value we put on our words—every word, all the time—because God does. He hates empty, fruitless words. This verse says that when we just talk a bunch of worthless, useless talk, we are actually in disobedience! We are disobeying His mandate to be fruitful, multiply, and take dominion with our words. Instead, we are wasting our time and our authority talking about things that do not matter. Again and again throughout the Bible, we are seeing how God takes every word we say very seriously.

Our words are spirit, and they are going to do something. When our words line up with His Word, they are not only spirit, but they are also filled with abundant and eternal life. When we say something vain or empty, however, our words are a mockery of the spiritual position and authority Jesus died to give us. Vain speaking will never bring Heaven to Earth or cause God's kingdom to come.

Vain speaking is what the devil loves, and for several reasons. The most obvious reason is that it displeases God and keeps us from declaring His will and Word in the Earth, but there is a more subtle deception going on here. When you speak vain words, words you don't really believe or mean, you will probably not suffer any consequences from it. It's not going to be fatal if you say something like, "I'm dying to go," because you don't believe what you are saying. However, what this will do is convince your spirit man that you don't believe every word you say. Over time, your heart gets accustomed to not believing what your mouth is saying.

Jesus said that you must believe in your heart what you say or pray with your mouth, and then you will have whatever you say. One of the principles of the law of confession is that your heart and your mouth must be in agreement for your words to carry power. When you speak vain words you don't mean, it causes your heart to no longer have faith in what your mouth is saying. It is a subtle way of causing your heart and your mouth to disconnect and disagree. Later, when you try to make an "I believe, I receive" type of faith statement, your faith in your own words is weak or nonexistent. Your heart can't believe what you are saying.

You may say, "Money, cometh to me now," but deep inside, your heart does not believe it. You have fallen into wishful thinking instead of faith-filled expectation. At that point, you have a bigger problem than needing money! The Word of God is as strong and reliable as ever, but your own word has become unreliable. Your heart doesn't trust what comes out of your mouth. That's not a spiritual condition you ever want to be in!

How do you heal the disconnect and disagreement that now exists between your heart and your mouth? How do you get your heart to believe your mouth? First, if you realize you've been saying a lot of stuff you don't really believe, repent—stop it—and then rejoice! You have just been delivered from the deception of the enemy. You can now use the law of confession as God intended you to use it. Second, ask the Father to cleanse your heart of all unbelief and bring your heart and mouth back into agreement (Psalm 51:10).

Third, stay focused on God's Word. The Bible tells us to meditate on God's Word day and night. If you do this you will recognize vain talk very quickly. The light of God's Word always exposes the works of darkness. The Word of God also will cleanse your heart and fill it with truth and increase your faith. Then whenever you speak, you will expect what you say to come to pass, and if you are saying something you don't want to happen, you will stop yourself and repent immediately. You will cancel those harmful words and release the truth and goodness of God instead.

One of Satan's most effective strategies against God's people is to convince them that their words don't matter. He doesn't want us to know the law of confession even exists. If we do find out about it, he tries to get us to think that our prayers and declarations of faith will not be affected by speaking vain words we don't believe from time to time. He will do anything he can to keep us from taking our words seriously and keeping our hearts and mouths from being in agreement with God's Word.

Now that you know this great deception, you need not fall prey to it! You can have the wonderful life God wants you to have by speaking what He says, believing your words are spirit and life, and allowing the Holy Spirit to correct you every time you begin to say something that is not what you really believe and want to come to pass.

Say What You Believe— Not What You Fear

Once you are in the kingdom of God, one of the first things you must learn is the law of confession: the creative power and eternal value of your words. As a believer, you are going to have to value your words in a new way.

We know the law of confession is true for the saved and the unsaved alike because confession is a law. When an unbeliever says something they believe, it comes to pass. When they say something they do not believe, it doesn't come to pass. Unbelievers have no idea that when they believe the doctor's report and start confessing it with their mouth, that disease is going to play out exactly the way the doctor and they have confessed. It can be a whole different story with believers.

As believers who understand "by His stripes we were healed" (1 Peter 2:4), we can overcome that negative doctor's report with God's Word on healing. Just like the law of lift supersedes the law of gravity, confessing what God says about our health supersedes what the doctor has said about it. His Word is Spirit and life and His spiritual words spoken in faith govern our natural lives.

Sometimes we have the tendency to blame someone else for what's going on in our lives. We say somebody else is our problem. Many of us have been trained to think that way, but it just isn't true. When we analyze it carefully, in most cases we find the main cause of our problem is less than two inches below our noses! We are just saying what we believe, and what we believe is not what we or God really want for us. We are saying something we should not say.

Job

Job was the richest man in the East because he had the blessing of God on his life. Even the devil testified about Job's success.

> And the LORD said unto Satan, Hast thou considered my servant Job, that there is none like him in the earth, a perfect and an upright man, one that feareth God, and escheweth evil?
>
> Then Satan answered the LORD, and said, Doth Job fear God for nought?

Hast not thou made an hedge about him, and about his house, and about all that he hath on every side? thou hast blessed the work of his hands, and his substance is increased in the land.

Job 1:8-10

Job had everything going for him, but something was not quite right. Let's read the rest of this discussion between the Lord and Satan about Job. Satan goes on to say,

But put forth thine hand now, and touch all that he hath, and he will curse thee to thy face.

And the LORD said unto Satan, Behold, all that he hath is in thy power; only upon himself put not forth thine hand. So Satan went forth from the presence of the LORD.

Job 1:11-12

We know what happened next. Job lost everything. His children were killed, his livestock were taken by enemies, and most of his servants were killed. Why? We know the Bible says in Proverbs 26:2 that a curse doesn't come without a cause. There was a reason all these terrible things happened to Job.

In verse 8, the Lord declared that Job was perfect and upright, a man who feared Him and turned away from evil. Then in verse 12, He told Satan that everything Job had was in his power, but He forbade him to touch Job himself. Here we see something very interesting. We can be righteous and still allow Satan to have power over what concerns us. We may be saved and going to Heaven, but if there is something not right it can open the door for the enemy to come in and wreak havoc in our lives.

I don't know about you, but I want to know just what it was that allowed the devil into Job's life. First, let's look at how Job reacted after this huge tragedy in his life. After he lost all his possessions and his children he said,

The LORD gave and the LORD hath taken away; blessed be the name of the LORD.

Job 1:21

Now that statement is in the Bible, and it is true that Job did say it, but what he said just flat-out was not true. The Lord didn't do anything to Job. The Bible hadn't been written when Job was alive, so he didn't know that the Lord only blesses His children (James 1:17) and never tempts them with evil (James 1:13). Job's statement reveals what he really believed in his heart, however. He believed the lie that the Lord might hurt him. What he did have right was his attitude of respect and honor for the Lord. He still blessed His name. He could have forsaken Him, but he didn't. The Lord was still his Lord, no matter what. That's why the Word says in verse 22,

In all this Job sinned not, nor charged God foolishly.

Job didn't sin or have a bad attitude, but he also didn't have a good understanding of the true nature and character of God. In the chapters that follow, Job begins to see where he went wrong in his thinking and believing. Early on, he recognizes what it was that allowed the devil to have access to what was important to him. The truth came right out of his mouth.

For the thing which I greatly feared is come upon me.

Job 3:25

Job admitted he had been in fear about his family and had been speaking that fear for some time, which gave Satan the opportunity to come in and steal his goods and kill his children and servants. Job realized that Satan is energized by our words of fear in the same way God is energized by our words of faith.

Through all his trials, Job grew to understand what he had done. He realized he still had a lot to learn and said to God,

Teach me, and I will hold my tongue: and cause me to understand wherein I have erred.

Job 6:24

Job had learned the hard way what God tells us in Proverbs 6:2:

Thou art snared with the words of thy mouth, thou art taken with the words of thy mouth.

In the end, God gave Job twice the children and servants and other wealth that he had lost because he stayed faithful and teachable. Job learned the law of confession the hard way—I believe God put his story in the Bible so that we would not have to. We can study the life of Job and learn not to speak words of fear. We are to speak words of faith in God and His promises.

A Matter of Life and Death

After reading what happened to Job, you can see that the importance of your words cannot be overstated. What you say can be a matter of life and death for you or someone else. During Job's trials and difficulties, God gave him a lecture concerning the law of confession.

> Knowest thou the ordinances of heaven? canst thou set the dominion thereof in the earth?
>
> Job 38:33

It is much clearer in *The Living Bible,* which reads,

> Do you know the laws of the universe and how the heavens influence the earth?
>
> Job 38:33 TLB

My paraphrase would be, "Do you know how the spiritual laws I have put in place affect the natural laws of this Earth?"

Many people blame God because they believe He has the last word in their lives. That makes God their problem. The Bible clears up this misunderstanding.

> Death and life are in the power of the tongue: and they that love it shall eat the fruit thereof.
>
> Proverbs 18:21

Notice this verse does not say that death and life are in the power of *God.* And it doesn't say that death and life are in the power of *Satan*. God has put the responsibility of life and death on what you say. It's your tongue, and it's up to you to control it. Neither God nor the devil can do anything without your permission.

Your mouth can destroy the dreams God has put in your heart. So say what you need to say, and then just be quiet. In the Old Testament, Joseph would have had a lot less trouble realizing his dream if he hadn't been so quick to tell his brothers about it. That got him sold into slavery (Genesis 37). So listen to the Holy Ghost. He'll tell you when you need to talk and when you should keep quiet. And when you do speak, don't say any more than He gives you peace to say.

Proverbs 18:21 says we can actually cause a death or save a life with our words, but it is deeper than that. Life and death consist of more than just breathing or not breathing. Life is the abundant life Jesus died to give us (John 10:10), and death is anything that separates us from that abundant life. It is not just a matter of whether or not we are physically alive or dead, it is the quality of life we live. Whether we live or die, thrive or barely survive, depends on our words.

As children, many of us grew up hearing negative confessions over us. "Watch out!" "You're not gonna make it." "That's too hard for you." "You're not big enough, smart enough, or strong enough." Most of our parents and teachers meant well, but they had no idea their words had such power over us. Many of us also heard these word curses from other kids who really wanted to hurt us.

As believers, we must look at where we are today and compare that with what other people have spoken over us. Chances are, we have been speaking the same things and allowed the enemy into our lives. We can change what we say and cancel out all the negative things that we or someone else have said about us.

David also learned the power of words. He said,

Set a watch, O LORD, before my mouth; keep the door of my lips.

Psalm 141:3

This verse says your lips are a door. That means the words you say can let things into your life or get things out of your life. David understood this and prayed for God to keep the door of his lips. He lived under the Old Covenant, when God did things for the Old Testament saints He won't now do for New Testament saints. Under the New Covenant, you are responsible for keeping the door of your own lips. God will not keep the door of your lips for you. He will teach you the law of confession in His Word, and He will show you how and why you should choose your words wisely, but He won't do it for you. It's up to you to take control of your mouth.

David also wrote,

I said, I will take heed to my ways, that I sin not with my tongue: I will keep my mouth with a bridle, while the wicked is before me.

Psalm 39:1

"The wicked" refers to Satan or demons. Demons are waiting on your mouth. They are perched nearby, whispering words of death and destruction in your ear, hoping you will speak them and give them permission to bring hell into your life. They know life and death are not in the power of God or the power of Satan. Life and death are in your power and are dependant on what you say. Demons will try to distract you or put a situation before you that will cause you to say the wrong thing. Their job is to get you to say something God wouldn't or didn't say.

Satan not only has kept the Church from using the law of confession for our good, but he has also kept our understanding darkened so we actually use this law to our own detriment. He has kept this law hidden from us because he knows when we begin to use it as God intends, he's in for a heap of trouble! People will be saved both spiritually and physically and believers all over the place will be living in abundant life—just like Job after he learned the power of his words.

Discovering the Mystery

We can learn from Job and refuse to speak anything that is not in line with what God has for us in His Word and what the Holy Spirit has revealed to us. We can use the law of confession as God intended us to use it: for good and not evil. But we must dig deep to understand the mystery concerning the law of confession. This law is one of the mysteries in the Bible that has been hidden *for* the Church not *from* the Church.

Mysteries are things that are beyond natural comprehension and must be spiritually known and understood. Jesus talked about these mysteries to the twelve.

> And the disciples came, and said unto him, Why speakest thou unto them in parables?
>
> He answered and said unto them, Because it is given unto you to know the mysteries of the kingdom of heaven, but to them it is not given.
>
> Matthew 13:10-11

As you know, a parable is a story that illustrates a truth. It doesn't come right out and state the principle or law it is demonstrating. The truth it tells is a mystery except to those who have spiritual ears to hear and spiritual eyes to see. Jesus taught a lot in parables because He was speaking to those who loved truth and would dig for the truth. He knew that the people who didn't really care about the truth would just hear a good story and walk away, but those seekers of truth who recognized Him as the Truth would uncover the mysteries in His parables and be changed by them.

As disciples of Jesus, we have to take hold of these mysteries so we can live in the truth He spoke. It's essential for us to be continually aware of the power of our words, so we can speak life wherever we go and refuse to speak words that will hurt other people or ourselves.

Keeping Quiet

If we understand what Paul was instructing the church at Ephesus to do, it will be a lot easier to keep our mouths shut when we are about to say something we shouldn't say.

> Let no corrupt communication proceed out of your mouth, but that which is good to the use of edifying, that it may minister grace unto the hearers.
>
> Ephesians 4:29

"Corrupt communication" is translated from the Greek words *sapro* and *logos*. We have seen the word *logos* before. *Logos* means words, either spoken or written. *Sapro* tells us what kind of words: "rotten, putrefied; worn out; of poor quality, bad, unfit for use, worthless."[1]

It's obvious we would never want to speak words that were rotten or putrid, but it really begins to cut out a lot of what we say when we realize that we don't want to speak any words that are "worthless," "worn out," or "unfit for use." How much of what we say on a daily basis falls into those categories? Are we saying things that are unnecessary and will bring no life to anyone or anything?

Paul instructed the saints at Ephesus, and us, to build up and minister grace to people. God has not called us to tear other people down. And by the way, that includes you! You are not to put yourself down, either. You are not to speak anything that God didn't say about you in His Word or that the Holy Spirit hasn't spoken directly to your heart about who you are and what you are called to do. There are times when you just have to keep quiet.

If thou hast done foolishly in lifting up thyself, or if thou hast thought evil, lay thine hand upon thy mouth.

Proverbs 30:32

Sometimes you have to physically put your hand over your mouth to stop anything rotten, putrefied, worn out, of poor quality, bad, unfit for use, or worthless from coming out. Your boss has made you angry. Your spouse has done something to make you jealous. Your teenager has you in a panic. And all you want to do in that moment is let out a mouthful of useless words that will do nothing but make the situation worse. That is when you have to shut your mouth. Put your hand over it if you have to! Don't say a thing until you have been with God and have lined your heart and mind up with His. By doing this, you will not speak the evil thoughts that were bombarding your mind during your crisis.

There are many other scriptures in Proverbs that tell you the importance of keeping your mouth shut at times.

Whoso keepeth his mouth and his tongue keepeth his soul from troubles.

Proverbs 21:23

He that keepeth his mouth keepeth his life: but he that openeth wide his lips shall have destruction.

Proverbs 13:3

In the multitude of words there wanteth not sin: but he that refraineth his lips is wise.

Proverbs 10:19

Solomon, the author of Proverbs and wisest man on Earth other than Jesus, certainly felt strongly that it was wise to not always speak your mind. He knew about the law of confession: that words are the most powerful, creative force, and if those words are evil and have evil intent, we should not be saying them.

In Mark, chapter 5, we read where Jesus demonstrated how keeping silent made the difference between life and death.

> And, behold, there cometh one of the rulers of the synagogue, Jairus by name; and when he saw him, he fell at his feet,
>
> And besought him greatly, saying, My little daughter lieth at the point of death: I pray thee, come and lay thy hands on her, that she may be healed; and she shall live.
>
> And Jesus went with him; and much people followed him, and thronged him.
>
> Mark 5:22-24

I want you to notice what Jairus was confessing. He said that if Jesus came and laid hands on his daughter, she would not only live but also be completely healed. This is a great beginning for Jairus. It looks like everything is going to be just fine for him because Jesus agreed with him and is going with him to his house to heal his daughter. But then something happens to stop Jesus in His tracks. A woman who had been bleeding for twelve years made her way through the crowd, grabbed ahold of Jesus' robe, and was healed instantly—and Jesus felt it. He immediately stopped, looked around, and asked, "Who touched my clothes?" (Mark 5:30).

Now if I were Jairus and my daughter was near death, this would not sit well with me! I would want Jesus' full attention. I would want Him to keep up the pace in following me home. As if the delay wasn't bad enough, right then one of Jairus' servants arrived to tell him that his daughter had already died and he should leave Jesus alone!

Jesus heard the servant's words.

> As soon as Jesus heard the word that was spoken, he saith unto the ruler of the synagogue, Be not afraid, only believe.
>
> Mark 5:36

Before Jairus could say anything or change his confession of faith, Jesus told him not to be afraid and to believe. Jairus did exactly what Jesus said and didn't say a word. He kept a guard over his mouth and like the woman with the issue of blood, he got his miracle too. When they got to Jairus' house, Jesus threw out the unbelievers who were mourning there and said, "The damsel is not dead, but sleepeth" (Mark 5:39). Those unbelievers laughed at Jesus, but He wasn't trying to impress anyone; He was operating in God's law of confession.

> And he took the damsel by the hand, and said unto her, Talitha cumi; which is, being interpreted, Damsel, I say unto thee, arise.

And straightway the damsel arose, and walked; for she was of the age of twelve years. And they were astonished with a great astonishment.

Mark 5:41-42

As always, Jesus received what He had said, and Jairus received what he had believed and spoken. He received because he did not speak any words of fear, anger, doubt, or unbelief when it looked like all hope was gone.

Like all of us who are believing God for something, Jairus had the opportunity to say the wrong thing at the wrong time, to destroy his confession of faith with fearful and unbelieving words. He had said the right thing when he first spoke to Jesus, confessing his faith in Jesus to heal his daughter, and he had to stick with that confession, no matter what happened afterward. When circumstances were totally against him, he kept silent and stuck with his former confession. As a result, he got the miracle he needed.

When you are working on a faith project, the enemy will always try to deceive you with lying circumstances, send people to disagree with your confession of faith, bring discouragement, and try to get you to say something you shouldn't say. Then he can take your words and cause "what you feared most" to come upon you. So never back off of your confession of faith! Stick to it no matter what is happening.

What is it that you shouldn't say?

Anything that goes against what God has said in your heart—by His Word or by His Spirit.

5

When Pressure Comes...Just Say No!

A s soon as you get the revelation of the law of confession and begin to walk in it, you are going to experience all kinds of pressure. The devil and his demons will work overtime to throw circumstances and unbelieving people in your path to try to get you to move away from your confession of faith in God and His Word. The world you live in is programmed to cause doubt and unbelief wherever you go. And your flesh might be your biggest challenge, especially if you are not used to living your life according to God's Word instead of just doing whatever feels good at the time. Your old, carnal nature is selfish, negative, often afraid, and easily offended. So you must be aware of these enemies to your creative words of faith and know how to handle them.

A World of Hate

Now the works of the flesh are manifest, which are these; Adultery, fornication, uncleanness, lasciviousness,

Idolatry, witchcraft, hatred, variance, emulations, wrath, strife, seditions, heresies,

Envyings, murders, drunkenness, revellings, and such like: of the which I tell you before, as I have also told you in time past, that they which do such things shall not inherit the kingdom of God.

Galatians 5:19-21

I once heard a story of a lady who said, "Preacher, you really did preach good tonight. You really cleaned out some cobwebs tonight."

The preacher replied, "Sister, come on back tomorrow night, and we're going to kill the spider."

We have to kill the spider because he is busy trying to build webs of hatred and bitterness in your life. Read verse 20 again—hatred is a work of the flesh. If you read the newspapers, surf the Internet blogs, or watch television news programs, you will catch on quickly that the world runs on hatred. It runs on hatred because that is the essence of Satan's character, and he is the god of this world (2 Corinthians 4:4).

Satan means "adversary."[1] He is the ultimate adversary, or one who opposes, because he is the adversary of God, who is love. Everything God does is motivated and energized by love. Everything Satan does is motivated and energized by hatred. He hates God, and he hates you. Jesus said in John 10:10 that Satan comes to kill, steal, and destroy you and everything that concerns you. He can do that if he can pressure you into speaking words of hate—any level of hate. Irritation. Frustration. Offense. Jealousy. Hurt. Unforgiveness and bitterness. These are his tools of destruction in your life.

> Be not deceived; God is not mocked: for whatsoever a man soweth, that shall he also reap.
>
> For he that soweth to his flesh shall of the flesh reap corruption; but he that soweth to the Spirit shall of the Spirit reap life everlasting.
>
> Galatians 6:7-8

Corruption is any form of destruction, and that is what you will reap if you sow hatred. How can you keep from speaking hateful words? It's easy when you meditate on the Cross and determine you will be like Jesus, not the world. Jesus hung on the cross for you, and He didn't deserve it. He hung there in agony while people insulted Him, spat on Him, tore His clothes, and cursed Him. What were the words He spoke? "Father, forgive them; for they know not what they do" (Luke 23:34).

Even Christians who hurt you or offend you may not understand what is behind their words or actions. They may have lost sight of the fact or never even heard that we don't wrestle with each other, but with the demonic forces of this world (Ephesians 6:12). Now that we are spiritual and God's children, we are to speak from the Spirit and the Word. We are not to speak words of hatred toward anyone. All our righteous anger and hatred should be focused only on the devil, his demons, and the sin in which he wants to ensnare us.

Some folks will try to get you to hate other folks who have different beliefs than yours or those who don't treat you the way you want to be treated. But Jesus told you to love your enemies and pray for those who persecute you and treat you badly (Matthew 5:44). Why? They cannot stop you from getting to your destiny. Only you can stop you by speaking words that do not line up with God's Word. No one person or group of people is your problem. Anyone who believes that is ignorant of the Word of God.

You need to get to the place where you have more confidence in the One who is for you than you do in the ones who are against you. If you train your heart to believe the Word and speak it out of your mouth, God will watch over that Word and make it good in your life. No one can stop God and His Word!

> He that saith he is in the light, and hateth his brother, is in darkness even until now.
>
> He that loveth his brother abideth in the light, and there is none occasion of stumbling in him.
>
> But he that hateth his brother is in darkness, and walketh in darkness, and knoweth not whither he goeth, because that darkness hath blinded his eyes
>
> 1 John 2:9-11

When it comes to talking religion and politics especially, even Christians can fall for the devil's trap and get to hating one another or hating the unbelievers who oppose their beliefs and point of view. This is not scriptural! The Bible says those who hate their brothers and sisters walk in darkness. They aren't getting any revelation. They don't know what they are doing or where they are going. They are stumbling around, not getting anywhere. They are not speaking God's will and Word into the Earth like they should—and they are miserable.

We are to love one another as Jesus loves us, and we are to show His love to those who don't know Him—and that includes anyone who disagrees with us!

> For ye see your calling, brethren, how that not many wise men after the flesh, not many mighty, not many noble, are called:
>
> But God hath chosen the foolish things of the world to confound the wise; and God hath chosen the weak things of the world to confound the things which are mighty;
>
> And base things of the world, and things which are despised, hath God chosen, yea, and things which are not, to bring to nought things that are:
>
> That no flesh should glory in his presence.
>
> 1 Corinthians 1:26-29

Do you see your calling? You are to confound the wise and the mighty with what they think is foolish and weak—your faith in God and His Word. The world will not think you are very smart because you believe God's Word over what your senses and your natural mind tell you. They will think you are a wimp because you rely on God instead of yourself. They will think you are an idiot because you don't hate anyone or compare yourself to others. But that's okay!

God chose you to "bring to nought things that are: That no flesh should glory in his presence." When the pressure comes and you are tempted to speak words of hate about someone but don't, you stop the enemy cold and bring glory to God. When you choose to do things God's way instead of the world's way, the result will confound anyone and anything that opposes God's Word. Your words will reveal the foolishness of those who are wise in their own eyes.

If you find yourself being pressured to get upset, angry, or enraged with anyone, stop it immediately. Forgive them and say what Jesus said, "Father, forgive them. They don't know what they're doing." Turn them over to Him. He knows what to do with them! And because you have sowed love and forgiveness, because you have spoken by the Spirit, you will reap life everlasting—here on Earth as well as in Heaven.

Get the Wisdom of God

When we were believing God for the money to buy the mall where our church is now located, I came under a lot of pressure. God had given me Joshua 1:3 as a supernatural seed to plant through my confession of faith.

Every place that the sole of your foot shall tread upon, that have I given unto you.

I walked over the property and took possession of the land in my spirit, proclaiming that every place I put my feet was mine, but the money to purchase the property had not come in yet. The lawyer called and said, "Pastor, where is the money?"

I said, "Well, you know, I believe I receive."

The lawyer wasn't impressed—not even a little bit—with my faith confession. "Believe you receive? What is that? We need the money. The developers want it now."

I thought I could have a moment of peace if I went down to the barbershop to get a haircut. I hadn't learned that the two places you don't want to go when you are believing for something are the barbershop and the beauty shop, if they are filled with unbelievers. They have enough unbelief there to take care of the whole neighborhood. Instead of getting some rest and relaxation, the pressure just got worse.

One of the barbers said, "Reverend, I hear y'all gonna buy that mall up there." He was winking at the other barbers.

I said, "Yeah."

What I should have said was, "Wait a minute. I already have it. God told me it was mine." They might have argued with me, but I should have stuck with what God had said. I have to admit I started backing up. I thought they wouldn't understand my confession and faith. Later, I realized I couldn't consider what some unbelievers or anybody else thought about what I said. The Bible says in Romans 3:4, "Let God be true, but every man a liar." I've got to say what God said, no matter what. I have to act according to His wisdom.

When you are in a pressure cooker, whether or not it's a life or death situation, you feel like it is a matter of life or death! At that point you have to confess the Word of God and stand on it.

I shall not die, but live, and declare the works of the LORD.

Psalm 118:17

Confessing what God says is the way to put spiritual law into motion in the natural realm, but first you have to find out what God is really saying about your situation. The law of confession doesn't work if you just go off and start confessing verses of Scripture that seem to apply. If you do this, you are in your own mind, not God's, and He's the only one who really knows the answer to your problem. You need His wisdom.

The Bible tells us in 1 Thessalonians 5:17 that we are to pray without ceasing, which means we are to be in constant communication with the Lord. When trouble arises and pressure mounts, we are to get His counsel and instruction before we say or do anything. Sometimes His answer makes perfect sense, but other times we don't see the wisdom in it until later.

When I had to get permission from the city to hold our church services in the mall, I prayed in tongues and God gave me some specific instructions that made no sense to my natural mind. He told me to go to the mayor's office and read the first four verses of Romans, chapter 13. So that Wednesday, I walked in to see our mayor, opened my Bible, and read the exact verses God had told me to read.

Let every soul be subject unto the higher powers. For there is no power but of God: the powers that be are ordained of God.

Whosoever therefore resisteth the power, resisteth the ordinance of God: and they that resist shall receive to themselves damnation.

For rulers are not a terror to good works, but to the evil. Wilt thou then not be afraid of the power? do that which is good, and thou shalt have praise of the same:

For he is the minister of God to thee for good. But if thou do that which is evil, be afraid; for he beareth not the sword in vain: for he is the minister of God, a revenger to execute wrath upon him that doeth evil.

Romans 13:1-4

The wisdom of God came through miraculously. I could never have figured out how to reach that mayor's heart and mind in the natural, but God knew. She granted my request that day. We got into the mall for our service that evening, and we've been there ever since.

I strongly exhort you to continually walk with the Lord, and when the pressure hits, just turn to Him to obtain His wisdom for whatever you are facing. If the pressure comes and you haven't been walking closely with the Lord, repent and get back in close fellowship with Him. Remember, He is faithful and just to forgive you and cleanse you from all unrighteousness (1 John 1:9), and He's waiting for you to wake up and hear what He has to say. Then you can use the law of confession by saying what He says, do what He instructs you to do, and overcome the pressure of your situation.

Build Yourself Up in the Word

Because your future is in the power of your tongue, you must weigh every word you are about to speak against the Word of God. When the Holy Spirit imparts a vision for your life, learn early on to speak only what God spoke to you—and only speak about it to those with whom God has given you peace. Again, the enemy, the world, and your flesh will exert every kind of pressure to stop you—and that means keeping you from *homologeo,* saying what God says, and instead speaking words of doubt and unbelief.

Professionals will get in your face and tell you that you don't know enough about their field and you can't possibly do what God has told you to do. There will be people with higher degrees of education who don't think you can operate successfully in their environment. Demons will introduce thoughts saying you are from the wrong side of town and no one will take you seriously. And then your flesh will point out all your faults and weaknesses.

When you find yourself in a situation where all hell has broken loose, it is probably because the enemy is pressuring you to doubt God's Word and speak words of unbelief. The most important thing you can do is get into God's Word, meditate on it continuously, and either speak words of faith or stand quietly in faith. But I will warn you, if you have not been spending time every day in God's Word and walking in it, when pressure comes, you are going to have a rougher time. The truth is, whatever is inside you when the crisis occurs is what is going to come out.

The best advice I can give you is to prepare for times of pressure by putting the Word in your heart daily and staying in an attitude of prayer. Then when the pressure comes, you will be full of the truth of God's Word and the power of the Holy Ghost. And since faith comes by hearing the Word of God (Romans 10:17) and is built up by praying in the Spirit (Jude 20), you will also be full of faith. No matter what comes against you, out of you will flow God's powerful, creative words to bring to pass His will for your life.

Someone who makes all of us feel a little better when we fail a test of faith and speak the wrong things is Peter. The story began when Jesus told the twelve,

> Then saith Jesus unto them, All ye shall be offended because of me this night: for it is written, I will smite the shepherd, and the sheep of the flock shall be scattered abroad.
>
> Matthew 26:31

Peter immediately declared he would never betray Jesus. He was very confident when there wasn't any pressure on Him!

> Peter answered and said unto him, Though all men shall be offended because of thee, yet will I never be offended.
>
> Jesus said unto him, Verily I say unto thee, That this night, before the cock crow, thou shalt deny me thrice.
>
> Peter said unto him, Though I should die with thee, yet will I not deny thee. Likewise also said all the disciples.
>
> Matthew 26:33-35

Peter said he would die for Jesus; he would never betray Him. He was making the right faith confession, wasn't he? In essence he was saying, "Jesus, I'm your man. If everyone else forsakes You, You know I'm with You." And that was what he honestly believed. He thought he was God's man of faith and power and superior to all other believers, but Jesus could see what was in Peter's heart. It showed up outside the high priest's palace.

Now Peter sat without in the palace: and a damsel came unto him, saying, Thou also wast with Jesus of Galilee.

But he denied before them all, saying, I know not what thou sayest.

And when he was gone out into the porch, another maid saw him, and said unto them that were there, This fellow was also with Jesus of Nazareth.

And again he denied with an oath, I do not know the man.

And after a while came unto him they that stood by, and said to Peter, Surely thou also art one of them; for thy speech bewrayeth thee.

Then began he to curse and to swear, saying, I know not the man. And immediately the cock crew.

Matthew 26:69-74

Peter didn't have the faith and courage he thought he had in his heart. Out of the abundance of his heart, his mouth spoke. Under pressure, he did exactly what he told Jesus he would never do. He even started cussing them out and saying, "I don't know this brother." After the cock crowed, Peter remembered what Jesus had prophesied about him, ran away, and wept.

After His resurrection, Jesus didn't condemn Peter. Instead, He gave him the opportunity to cancel his words of denial and be restored.

So when they had dined, Jesus saith to Simon Peter, Simon, son of Jonas, lovest thou me more than these? He saith unto him, Yea, Lord; thou knowest that I love thee. He saith unto him, Feed my lambs.

He saith to him again the second time, Simon, son of Jonas, lovest thou me? He saith unto him, Yea, Lord;

thou knowest that I love thee. He saith unto him, Feed my sheep.

He saith unto him the third time, Simon, son of Jonas, lovest thou me? Peter was grieved because he said unto him the third time, Lovest thou me? And he said unto him, Lord, thou knowest all things; thou knowest that I love thee. Jesus saith unto him, Feed my sheep.

John 21:15-17

Peter had denied Jesus three times, so three times Jesus asked Peter, "Do you love Me?" and three times Peter made the positive confession that he loved Him. From that time on, Peter was more diligent about God's Word. We know this because at the end of his life, the last thing he wrote in his second epistle was an exhortation to believers to remain steadfast in God's Word (2 Peter 3:15-18). From the Day of Pentecost until his death, Peter became very bold in preaching the gospel and eventually was martyred for his refusal to deny Jesus as his Lord.

Peter's story gives hope to all of us to continue in faith when we fail the Lord. It reveals God's unending grace and mercy toward us. So no matter where you are or what spiritual condition you are in right now, you can turn it all around just like Peter did. You can change your confession and begin to build yourself up in the Word of God.

As a spiritual being, your spiritual life depends on spiritual food, which is God's Word. His words are Spirit and they are life, so begin eating right now! Fill yourself up so that when you are squeezed by the pressures of life, only truth and goodness will come out of your mouth.

The Right Seed Brings the Right Fruit

When I am fighting a battle in the spirit, I pay special attention to what is going into my spirit and my soul. I know that whatever goes in is going to come out under pressure, and I want only good fruit produced from my life.

> Not that which goeth into the mouth defileth a man; but that which cometh out of the mouth, this defileth a man.
>
> Then came his disciples, and said unto him, Knowest thou that the Pharisees were offended, after they heard this saying?
>
> But he answered and said, Every plant, which my heavenly Father hath not planted, shall be rooted up.
>
> Matthew 15:11-13

Fruit is the physical manifestation of the seeds that have been sown in your heart. In this passage of Scripture, Jesus tells you that your words can defile you. He said your words plant something in your heart, which grows into a tall tree with deep roots. A tree of truth will hold you steady when pressure comes, but a tree of deception and lies will cause you to fall and fail and must be pulled out by the roots.

In Luke 8:11 Jesus said, "The seed is the word of God." He is the Sower of the Word, but the devil is the sower of lies. When you speak, you will speak from the tree that has been planted and has grown deep roots in your heart. Those words are the fruit that reflect either the truth of God's Word or the lies and deception of the enemy inside you.

A tree of lies could be the perception you have of yourself. If you do not see yourself as God sees you, if your perception of yourself does not line up with God's Word, you know you must allow the Holy Spirit to pull out the evil tree as you plant the good seed in your heart. You need to put some new seed in there so you can be free and speak and walk in God's great plan for your life.

God wants to expose everything in your heart that doesn't come from Him or agree with His Word. That's what He did with the Israelites when He took them through the wilderness.

And thou shalt remember all the way which the LORD thy God led thee these forty years in the wilderness, to humble thee, and to prove thee, to know what was in thine heart, whether thou wouldest keep his commandments or no.

Deuteronomy 8:2

The children of Israel had some trees of evil in their hearts that needed to be pulled out before they could enter their Promised Land. He knew that once their hearts were purged of idolatry and unbelief and filled with faith in Him and His Word, they would be able to overcome all pressure and all obstacles and take the land He had given them.

The same is true for you. If you find you are not able to realize your dreams or you are continually battling discouragement and depression, ask the Holy Spirit to reveal any evil trees of lies in your heart.

You Live From Within

Keep thy heart with all diligence; for out of it are the issues of life.

Put away from thee a froward mouth, and perverse lips
put far from thee.

Proverbs 4:23-24

Here you can see the relationship between what is in
your heart, what you speak, and how your life goes. As a
child of God, you speak and act according to the Word and
the Spirit within your spirit. You do not live according to the
world, the forces of darkness, or your flesh—these are
outside of you. That's why the enemy tries to plant seeds of
destruction and death into your heart. Satan understands
that you live from the inside, so if he can get you to believe
a lie in your heart, that will cause you to talk crosswise with
the Word of God and sabotage what God wants to do. The
enemy pressures you from the outside, so you have to be
full of the Word and the Spirit on the inside.

How do you know when Satan has planted a tree of lies
and deception in your heart? All you have to do is examine
the fruit in your life. Do you produce righteousness, peace,
and joy in the Holy Ghost; or do you produce self-right-
eousness, agitation, and depression? Are you at peace or
filled with anxiety? Are you driven or do you flow easily in
God's grace? Are you angry a lot of the time or do you
forgive and move on? Is your life filled with blessing or
turmoil, chaos, and confusion? Maybe you never seem to
have enough money to pay your bills. Are you noticing "lack
fruit" in your life? If that is the case, you can be sure the
enemy has planted images of poverty and lack inside you.
These images may be so subtle that only the illumination of
God's Word and Spirit will expose them.

Have you heard the expression, "You can't see the forest for the trees"? The seed Satan plants is designed to grow into a tree of lies that obscures God's truth. You can read the Word, look right at it, and still not see who you really are in Christ Jesus and all He has for you. But Jesus said in Matthew 15:13 that every plant God did not plant would be uprooted. He will expose that tree of blindness and pull it out by the roots as you abide in God's Word.

> The entrance of thy words giveth light; it giveth understanding unto the simple.
>
> Psalm 119:130

The Word of God always shines its light on the works of darkness and exposes the evil plants of the enemy. Then God pulls them out by His Spirit and His Word. You can cut away the bad fruit on the outside of you year after year, but that bad fruit is going to keep showing up until you surrender the whole issue to God, fill yourself with the good seed of His Word, and allow His Spirit to pull out that evil tree once and for all. Every trace of that bad seed has to be eliminated, or else the tree will grow back and bad fruit will continue to manifest.

God doesn't operate in halfway measures. Remember when Jesus cursed the fig tree? It dried up *from the root.* God's plan is to do exactly the same thing in your heart, to remove all the evidence of Satan's seed from your life and plant the good seed of His Word in your heart. Then you will become what God says you are:

Blessed is the man that walketh not in the counsel of the ungodly, nor standeth in the way of sinners, nor sitteth in the seat of the scornful.

But his delight is in the law of the LORD; and in his law doth he meditate day and night.

And he shall be like a tree planted by the rivers of water, that bringeth forth his fruit in his season; his leaf also shall not wither; and whatsoever he doeth shall prosper.

Psalm 1:1-3

You will be like a tree planted by a mighty, life-giving river. You will produce fruit of righteousness, peace, and joy. You will overcome any pressure that comes against you, and everything you do will prosper.

Training Your Spirit

When pressure comes, if your spirit has been trained to believe every word that comes out of your mouth, you are already halfway to total victory. Your trained spirit is purged of evil roots because you have stopped being complacent about the words you speak. You diligently watch what's coming out of your mouth and make sure you are saying exactly what you believe in your heart, and what you believe in your heart lines up completely with God's Word.

You might catch yourself saying, "That blows my mind." Do you really want your mind to be blown? Think about this, because you probably say things like that every day. Yes, it's just an expression; but remember, saying those things will train your spirit not to believe what you say.

Then, when you want to believe in your heart what you say with your mouth, you will struggle with doubt and unbelief. To keep this from happening, you must continually abide in God's Word. You must be as serious about your words as God is about His words.

> I will worship toward thy holy temple, and praise thy name for thy lovingkindness and for thy truth: for thou hast magnified thy word above all thy name.
>
> Psalm 138:2

God is so committed to His Word that when He speaks, He places Himself under the authority of the words He spoke. He is a God of integrity. You won't ever get Him to violate His Word. If He has promised something to you in His Word, He gives Himself to it completely. That is the kind of integrity you want your heart to have and your mouth to speak. Then your spirit will always believe what you say.

When we really start to believe that everything we say will come to pass, it is amazing what can happen. There was a meeting where two speakers, Jerry Savelle and Charles Capps, were scheduled in the same session. Jerry was first, and as he went up to speak, he asked the moderator how much time he had. The moderator said he had an hour. Then Jerry asked who was speaking after him and the moderator told him Charlie was. Jerry answered, "Well, I'll tell you what, I'm going to take Charlie's time too," and he laughed. He was joking.

Jerry started speaking and looked at his watch. He had plenty of time. He continued speaking and looked at his watch again—still plenty of time. After he'd spoken a while more, he looked at his watch another time and realized that his watch had stopped. He asked, "What time is it?"

The moderator said, "Jerry, you have taken all of your time and all of Charlie's time." Jerry began to apologize.

Charles Capps got up and very graciously said, "Let me just say one thing. Jerry has trained his spirit to believe that everything he says will come to pass."

Jerry was a good man, and his spirit had been trained to believe every word he spoke. So his statement about taking Charlie's time had gone down into his heart and become part of the good root of faith and believing there. His words were spirit and life, and they manifested just what he said, even though he had spoken them in jest. This is a perfect illustration of the power of having our spirits trained to believe what we say—and the respect we need to have for that power.

Operating in the law of confession is going to bring pressure. We know that for certain! And if we are going to be all God created us to be and do all He created us to do, we must learn to handle all kinds of pressure. Do you see how effective we can be in handling pressure if we seek God's wisdom for every decision, build ourselves up in His Word, plant the right seed in our hearts, pull out every evil root, grow deep roots of truth, and train our spirits to believe every word we say? We could declare Joshua 1:5 like this: "No pressure shall be able to stand before us all the days of our lives!"

6

A New Education for a New Creation

Believers will come to our church, hear the Word of God being preached and taught, and after awhile they want to go on one of our evangelism outreaches. While they are telling people about Jesus, they will hear things coming out of their mouths they had no idea were inside them. Why does this happen? Seeds of truth that were planted in them had grown roots, and out of the abundance of their hearts their mouths spoke. This is the fruit of the right education.

The education we get in the world can be very beneficial. We can learn all about the profession God has called us to pursue. Today, there are great institutions of learning and vast resources available to us from which to learn about anything. If we don't have a personal computer with access to the Internet, every city has a public library with computers and Internet access as well as a multitude of books to read on just about any subject.

What I just described is what secular education is about: information and knowledge, mostly about the material world. However, believers need another education, and without this education they will certainly perish.

> My people are destroyed for lack of knowledge: because thou hast rejected knowledge, I will also reject thee, that thou shalt be no priest to me: seeing thou hast forgotten the law of thy God, I will also forget thy children.
>
> Hosea 4:6

This verse is not talking about the knowledge of this world; it is talking about the knowledge of God. When knowing Him is the focus of our lives, all other knowledge is turned to wisdom. In other words, we know what to do with the information we have because the Creator of all things is our teacher and leader.

> The fear of the LORD is the beginning of wisdom: and the knowledge of the holy is understanding.
>
> Proverbs 9:10

> But of him are ye in Christ Jesus, who of God is made unto us wisdom, and righteousness, and sanctification, and redemption.
>
> 1 Corinthians 1:30

Jesus is made unto us wisdom. We are in Him, He is in us, and that means we have His wisdom. We can know by the Spirit and the Word what to do with the information and facts that we learn.

What I have been describing to you is a spiritual education. This is the stuff you have to learn in order to take dominion, be fruitful and multiply, and guard all God has given you to guard. You cannot operate successfully in the law of confession, which is a spiritual law, unless you have a spiritual education.

Spiritual education only comes on the spirit level. It doesn't come on the natural level. It's good to have skills and information, but to defeat the enemy and accomplish what God has called you to accomplish, you will need more than that. You must have the heart and mind of God. Then you will have His wisdom to use all the other information and knowledge you have—and what you speak will carry His will and creative power.

Your Family of God

To receive the spiritual education God wants to give you, you must get yourself in a good local church, your personal family of God. Although hearing the Word of God is one of the most important aspects of being involved in a local body of believers, your spiritual education involves more than that. The church isn't just a place to come and sit. Nor is it just a place to come and worship and praise and shout. Your church is your training ground for taking dominion, being fruitful, multiplying, and guarding what God called you to guard.

Some folks expect the preacher to get in the pulpit and cry and whoop and entertain them. They think that's real spiritual. That makes no more sense than when I was a little kid and I would look at the fancy shoes my preacher had sticking out from under his robe and think, *Boy, if I had some of those shoes, I bet I could preach too.* I thought those shoes were what made him acceptable to God. I wasn't the only one confused about preachers in those days. Some folks thought a preacher wasn't acceptable unless he was poor, and other folks thought he wasn't acceptable unless he was driving a Cadillac. None of those thoughts had any truth in them!

There are a lot of bad traditions and silly ideas and doctrines to overcome in churches, but the corporate fellowship of believers is the format God chose to grow us up and educate us in spiritual matters. We will only get a true spiritual education in the company of a community of believers.

> And let us consider one another to provoke unto love and to good works:
>
> Not forsaking the assembling of ourselves together, as the manner of some is; but exhorting one another: and so much the more, as ye see the day approaching.
>
> Hebrews 10:24-25

Today, many believers have given up going to church. They believe they can stay home and watch a few church services or Bible teachers on television and still grow in the Lord. They will say, "Sunday morning, channel 17, is my church." They are deceived and trying to deceive others because they don't interact with any of those people on TV.

Yes, they may be provoked to love and good works in a message, but who is there to hold them accountable for it? With whom are they going to walk it out? When they begin saying things that go against what the Word of God has to say, who is going to catch it and call them on it? When the pressure hits and the bottom falls out from underneath them, who is going to be there to encourage them in the Word and pray them through? Who is going to marry them and bury them and be there for them in those turning points in life? That televangelist is not going to spend an hour on the phone with them, and all the people in that television church service are strangers to them.

Your local family of believers is the primary place for you to receive your spiritual education. Just like you learned from your natural parents and brothers and sisters, you get your spiritual education from your spiritual parents and brothers and sisters. You then pass what you learn on to your spiritual sons and daughters. Sometimes you learn what not to do, but you always learn something because Romans 8:28 says God works all things for your good when you believe Him and walk according to His purpose—and He has purposed for you to be connected with other believers in a local church or fellowship.

The local church is where you learn the Word, hear from God, learn how to walk and move in the gifts of the Spirit, begin to realize and walk in your gifts and ministry, and grow up in Christ. You can't walk in the law of confession successfully without the regular fellowship of other believers and the pastoral care of leaders in your family of God.

How do you connect with a local body of believers? You go where God tells you to go because He knows you better than you know yourself. He knows the people you need to rub up against to get all those rough edges smoothed down. He knows the pastors and teachers who will bring the Word He has for you. He knows where you will grow in your gifts and callings, where you will be edified and built up. And He knows where you will be challenged to keep your heart filled with the Word, your mouth speaking only what God says, and your feet in God's will. This is how you will be conformed to the image of Jesus and be able to do what you were created to do.

If you are not going to church because you have been offended and hurt, you need to know right now that the perfect church is in Heaven, not on Earth. No matter what church you attend, there will come a time when you are going to find fault with the pastor and the members. Wherever we are in the Lord, we are all still contending with the enemy, the world, and our flesh. From time to time we let each other down and miss it—even pastors! That is why the Christian life is founded on forgiveness not condemnation and criticism.

One of the greatest confessions of faith you will utter is, "I forgive you." And when you believe what you say, your heart and soul will be free from all judgment and negativity toward your brothers and sisters. You can walk in love and not compromise what you know to be true. You can learn that in difficult situations in the church. Think about this: If Jesus was perfected in suffering, how will you be perfected?

For it became him, for whom are all things, and by whom are all things, in bringing many sons unto glory, to make the captain of their salvation perfect through sufferings.

Hebrews 2:10

Beloved, think it not strange concerning the fiery trial which is to try you, as though some strange thing happened unto you:

But rejoice, inasmuch as ye are partakers of Christ's sufferings; that, when his glory shall be revealed, ye may be glad also with exceeding joy.

1 Peter 4:12-13

The kind of suffering these verses are talking about is not physical. They are talking about relationships with people, and many of those people are fellow believers who are not perfect just like you are not perfect. We are all in the process of being perfected and conformed to the image of Jesus Christ, and that means we are going to have to weather some storms, clear up some misunderstandings, practice a lot of forgiveness, and make certain that our confession does not waiver from God's Word no matter what has been said or done to us. This is one of the most important aspects of our spiritual education!

A Collision of Educations

God delivered the children of Israel out of the bondage of Egypt through signs, wonders, and miracles. You would think that would have given His people a tremendous education in how spiritual laws govern natural laws. But what influenced them was what had been planted in their hearts during their centuries of slavery in Egypt. When Moses went up to meet with God on Mount Sinai, He stayed longer than the Israelites thought he would, and they became restless. They spoke and acted from what was in their hearts, which was the idolatry and selfishness they had learned in Egypt.

> And when the people saw that Moses delayed to come down out of the mount, the people gathered themselves together unto Aaron, and said unto him, Up, make us gods, which shall go before us; for as for this Moses, the man that brought us up out of the land of Egypt, we wot not what is become of him.
>
> And Aaron said unto them, Break off the golden earrings, which are in the ears of your wives, of your sons, and of your daughters, and bring them unto me.
>
> And all the people brake off the golden earrings which were in their ears, and brought them unto Aaron.
>
> And he received them at their hand, and fashioned it with a graving tool, after he had made it a molten calf: and they said, These be thy gods, O Israel, which brought thee up out of the land of Egypt.
>
> And when Aaron saw it, he built an altar before it; and Aaron made proclamation, and said, To morrow is a feast to the LORD.
>
> And they rose up early on the morrow, and offered burnt offerings, and brought peace offerings; and the people sat down to eat and to drink, and rose up to play.
>
> Exodus 32:1-6

When Moses came back down the mountain after receiving the Ten Commandments, he found the people had made a golden calf. Why a calf? They had seen gods like that in Egypt and had brought that idolatry into the wilderness on the inside of them. It had been deposited in their hearts in Egypt. That had been their education, whether they realized it or not. Now God had brought them out of Egypt, but He needed to get Egypt out of them. After receiving the Ten Commandments from God, Moses' spiritual education collided with that golden calf of worldly education!

In the same way, when we get saved we need to be re-educated to spiritual truths, and sometimes that causes collisions between what we have thought and passionately held to in the past and what God says in His Word. We must change the way we think, speak, and act from the way the enemy, the world, and our old, sinful nature educated us. We must submit ourselves to the Word of God and be transformed.

> I beseech you therefore, brethren, by the mercies of God, that ye present your bodies a living sacrifice, holy, accept-able unto God, which is your reasonable service.
> And be not conformed to this world: but be ye transformed by the renewing of your mind, that ye may prove what is that good, and acceptable, and perfect, will of God.
>
> Romans 12:1-2

When the Word of God confronts your old man and you must turn from that old belief or passion to embrace the truth, you feel like a living sacrifice! There is often a colli-sion between what is known and familiar and what is new and foreign. The children of Israel were familiar with and used to the Egyptian gods, but they were frightened of the

God of Moses. They needed to be educated in true spirituality, to grow in the knowledge of Him, so they could trust God and begin to speak and act from hearts following after God.

When things didn't go their way, the children of Israel spoke and acted out of what was in their hearts, which was in total disagreement with the Word of God. You don't want to react the way they did, and God has given you His Word so you can act differently. He desires His Word to be so established in your heart that when things don't go the way you thought they would, the Word is the only thing that can come out of your mouth. His Word enables you to conduct the affairs of your life with wisdom and joy.

All of us have those times when we have to choose whether we will believe and live by the Bible or by what we have been taught or thought to be true in the past. For example, I did not grow up in a church where they told me that what I said determined where I was going in life. They told me that "the man" was my problem, or that "the devil made me do it." They never said my life was my responsibility and that with my words, I create my world.

Also, when I was growing up the enemy tried to convince me that the Word of God was not for me. He put people in my life that said the white man wrote the Bible, and if I followed the Bible I would stay in bondage. I know many people of color are under that deception today. How did they get there? Their leaders were deceived and taught them the same lies. Some may have done it maliciously, but others were deceived and believed what they were teaching.

If you had known me back then, you might have heard me say, "Oh, this Book isn't for us black folk. The white man just wrote this Book to keep us in bondage." But the day came when I had to make a choice. I became born again and as I began to study the Scriptures, I was confronted with the truth of God's Word and an educational collision took place in my life. I saw that when the Bible said "whosoever," it meant anyone of any color, background, or culture. And when I began to really study the history of the Bible, I discovered it was not written by a certain ethnic group of people but it was inspired (God breathed) by the Holy Ghost!

I thank God I chose to believe God's Word over anything else I had been taught, and you will too. It delivered me from everything, from lack and debt, to sickness and low self esteem. When you find yourself in the middle of a conflict between your natural education and your spiritual education, between what your senses and your carnal mind tell you and what God tells you, it helps to remember that God's Word is truth and the controlling factor in every situation. Jesus said "The words that I speak unto you, they are Spirit and they are life" (John 6:63). The natural world is governed by the more powerful world of the spirit.

Make Your Tree Good

I know you want to be like that tree planted near the river of living water in Psalm 1:1-3, who bears good fruit in season and whose leaf never withers. That is why you are reading this book! Most times, the reason some evil things show up in our lives is that all the deposits in our hearts have not been of God. Out of the abundance of our hearts we can speak both good and bad, both life and death into our lives. Now Jesus is telling us it is time to make your tree and your fruit good.

> Either make the tree good, and his fruit good; or else make the tree corrupt, and his fruit corrupt: for the tree is known by his fruit.
>
> O generation of vipers, how can ye, being evil, speak good things? for out of the abundance of the heart the mouth speaketh.
>
> A good man out of the good treasure of the heart bringeth forth good things: and an evil man out of the evil treasure bringeth forth evil things.
>
> But I say unto you, That every idle word that men shall speak, they shall give account thereof in the day of judgment.
>
> For by thy words thou shalt be justified, and by thy words thou shalt be condemned.
>
> Matthew 12:33-37

Jesus uses legal terms in these verses. He is talking about verdicts in a court of law. We know that the word "justified" means acquitted or set free to prosper in every area of life, and condemned means to be put in bondage. Unless you went to a really good Christian school, I'm certain you never received the teaching that the spiritual law of confession governs your natural life and determines your eternal life. The Bible tells us that on the Day of Judgment, we will give account for our words. For example, if you have confessed Jesus as your Lord and Savior, His blood and your testimony will justify you.

"Thou shall be saved" from eternal separation from God (see Romans 10:9). These words are the most important fruit that could ever come from your lips! Fruit represents the manifestation of the seed of the Word of God.

Jesus also said in verse 34 of Matthew 12 that out of the abundance of your heart you will speak. If you want your words to be pleasing to God and life-giving to yourself and others, you must fill your heart with good things. If you have been speaking negatively and have had a bad attitude, you can make your tree good and produce good fruit by simply planting the Word of God into your heart. When you are transformed by the Word on the inside, your mouth will speak good things to the outside—and your life will be blessed and productive!

You are a spiritual and a natural being, but your spirit was created to govern your soul, your body and the circumstances of your life. That is why it is imperative that you get a spiritual education in God's Word and play the role you were destined by God to play in transforming this world for the Kingdom.

7

Made in His Image

One of the main things all Christians have to learn when we are born again is that we are a three-part being: spirit, soul, and body. Your spirit is who you really are—your eternal self—and you are made in the image and likeness of your Father and Creator, God, Who is a Spirit. You are connected to Him by your spirit, and you are connected to the Earth realm by your body.

Your body is not you. It houses you. You are a spirit and your spirit lives in your physical body. The Greek word for body is *soma,* which means a physical or corporeal body.[1] What makes your physical body alive? It is your spirit inside it. The moment your spirit leaves your body, your body dies. Your body is a shadow of what your spirit looks like. Your spirit has eyes, fingers, a tongue, and even feelings (Luke 16:23-25)—all of this without your body. Yet we think it is the other way around. Just think: if your physical body looks so good, imagine how good-looking your spirit is!

Your body is supposed to obey you because it is a slave of the real you, which is a spirit. This is another spiritual fact you were probably not taught in school, where the emphasis is on your mental, emotional, and physical person. It's good to know how your brain, emotions, and body work, but all of these things are subject to your spirit. If you are going to act like God, you must live from your spirit because He is a Spirit. The book of Ephesians tells us, "Be ye therefore followers of God, as dear children." That word "followers" is where we get our word "imitate."[2]

We are made in God's image, so we are spirit beings. Because the spirit realm governs the natural realm, our spirit will govern our soul and body. Furthermore, the spiritual laws that govern our spirit also supersede the natural laws that govern our soul and body. Therefore, the law of confession, which is a spiritual law, will govern both our spiritual and natural lives. For example, Jesus' one word, "Come," enabled Peter to walk on water in Matthew 14:29. That word went right into Peter's heart, he believed it, acted on it, by faith overcame the law of gravity, and Peter made his famous walk on the waves of the Sea of Galilee.

Do you see how the Church is behind in this? From the very beginning God created us to do things like supersede natural laws and dominate our circumstances. We have not been living in the fullness of what Jesus died to give us. But from now on, I decree joy, peace, and the fullness of the blessing be established in every area of your life.

Back to the Garden

In the beginning God created the heaven and the earth.

And the earth was without form, and void; and darkness was upon the face of the deep. And the Spirit of God moved upon the face of the waters.

And God said, Let there be light: and there was light.

Genesis 1:1-3

God, who is a Spirit, spoke things and they came to be. He had control over this physical world and in the verses that follow, He used His Words to speak trees, plants, animals, birds, and fish into the Earth. After everything was finished, He made human beings.

And God said, Let us make man in our image, after our likeness: and let them have dominion over the fish of the sea, and over the fowl of the air, and over the cattle, and over all the earth, and over every creeping thing that creepeth upon the earth.

So God created man in his own image, in the image of God created he him; male and female created he them.

Genesis 1:26-27

God gave us dominion, or management and stewardship, over the Earth and everything in it. He took His hands off all He created and turned it over to Adam and Eve, putting human beings in charge of the Earth.

And God blessed them, and God said unto them, Be fruitful, and multiply, and replenish the earth, and subdue it: and have dominion over the fish of the sea, and over the fowl of the air, and over every living thing that moveth upon the earth.

Genesis 1:28

The Hebrew word for "replenish" is *male* (pronounced maw-lay), and it means, "to fill."[5] This word carries the idea that human beings were to complete what God had started. They were to stock the Earth with an abundance of people who carried His presence and restore the planet to its former fullness—what it had been before Genesis 1:2. They were to act like God.

God had not created the Earth to be dark, without form, and void. Many scholars believe that happened with Lucifer's fall. According to Jesus in Luke 10:18, Lucifer (now called Satan) was cast out of Heaven and hit the Earth like a bolt of lightening. Because he was an archangel and extremely powerful, the impact he had on the Earth when he hit was probably cataclysmic, like a meteor colliding with the planet. That's when everything went dark and cold, and all living things died.

Jesus also gave us a picture of the spiritual condition of Satan. He destroys and devastates everything he touches. He brings cold and darkness wherever he goes because he opposes God, Who is love and light and makes all things good.

In Genesis 1:3, God began to restore the Earth with His words. Then He made us in His image and gave us the mandate to complete the work of replenishing the Earth.

And the LORD God formed man of the dust of the ground, and breathed into his nostrils the breath of life; and man became a living soul.

And the LORD God planted a garden eastward in Eden; and there he put the man whom he had formed.

Genesis 2:7-8

Notice what God did. He created a man in His own image, a spirit like Himself, but He also put man's spirit in a body that was formed from the Earth. This connected human beings to the Earth in a profound way. He created them to have perfect fellowship with Him, to walk in His glory and possess His nature. They were to reproduce until the whole world was replenished with spirit beings who carried His presence and glory. The whole Earth would be like the Garden of Eden. That was God's original plan and it never has changed.

The last part of verse 7 says, "Man became a living soul." What makes your soul alive? Your spirit! You are really a speaking spirit who is told to present your body "as a living sacrifice" in Romans 12:1. What part of you presents your body? Again, it is your spirit. Your spirit is supposed to be the control center of your life.

The next verse in Romans gives you more details about the spiritual challenge to control your mind, emotions, and body.

Do not be conformed to this world (this age), [fashioned after and adapted to its external, superficial customs], but be transformed (changed) by the [entire] renewal of your mind [by its new ideas and its new attitude], so that you may prove [for yourselves] what is the good and acceptable and perfect will of God, even the thing which is good and acceptable and perfect [in His sight for you].

Romans 12:2 AMP

You cannot let yourself be squeezed or conformed into the mold of this world. Renewing the mind means getting rid of the "stinkin' thinkin'" of the world. You can no longer say, "Hey Man, if it feels good, do it," because the Word of God says you don't live by your carnal feelings anymore. You live by the Spirit and must crucify that old flesh.

> But the fruit of the Spirit is love, joy, peace, longsuffering, gentleness, goodness, faith,
>
> Meekness, temperance: against such there is no law.
>
> And they that are Christ's have crucified the flesh with the affections and lusts.

Galatians 5:22-24

When temptation presents itself, instead of "doing what feels good" to your flesh, out of the abundance of your heart you will say, "Excuse me, but I'm a spirit who lives by *the* Spirit. I curse any inordinate affection or lust in my flesh and command it to die, and I declare that Jesus reigns in me—spirit, soul, and body. It's no longer I who live, but Christ, the Anointed One, lives in me (Galatians 2:20). He empowers me right now to say and do the right thing. Hallelujah!"

What did you just do? You went back to the Garden! You acted like God! You chose to live in the fullness of what Jesus provided for you, and you took dominion over that which was trying to ensnare you and trap you in sin. You replenished the Earth with more of the presence and power of God.

And you did all this with your words.

Your Words Control Your Life

By your words, you will either act like God or the devil. You will either express the will and Word of God or the deception and lies of the devil. Once you have that firmly established, you won't care what people say to you or about you because you know who God says you are and you are determined only to say what He says about you. You know what He says you can have and can do, and that is your confession of faith.

When you begin to operate in the law of confession, you may have problems with other people simply because you haven't built a track record of success. Sometimes you have to stick your neck out in faith, trust God to perform His Word, and watch the miracles happen a few times before you really become fully assured inside that what you say is going to happen because it is God's Word. There are times when you may feel silly, but that is just another collision between your natural education and your spiritual education. Keep pressing on because you were created to act this way.

After awhile this behavior will become easier and feel more comfortable. You will come to have faith in every word you speak. When a situation arises, you will get God's wisdom on it, speak His Word and will, and then go on to something else because you know your words are going to work exactly as you spoke them. This is how God created you to function in taking dominion over the Earth and replenishing it. This is acting like Him.

Typically, people aren't walking in this law of confession, not even in the Church. People say all kinds of crazy stuff, and you'll even hear church folk saying, "My feet are killing me," or "Girl, I'm just dying to go." You know they aren't dying and their feet aren't killing them. So why did they say that? They obviously don't believe a word they are saying and are training their hearts never to trust their mouths. They are hindering everything God wants to do in the Earth through them, for them, and in them.

If church folk got serious about what the Word says about their words, they would start taking everything they said a lot more seriously. Now, whenever I teach this message I will get this response from some people, "Pastor Winston, you're trying to put me in bondage."

My answer to them is simple, "No, you've already put yourself in bondage if you're not speaking what God says and training your spirit to believe what you say. There's no way you are going to take dominion or replenish anything the way you are talking because your words are not consistently lined up with God's Word. You must act like God to get God's results, and God doesn't talk faith one minute and say things He doesn't believe or mean the next."

Many times a brother or sister will come to me and say, "I just don't know, Pastor. Every month it's the same old same old. Never enough. Always scraping by. Tell me what to do."

Listen to what they just said to me: "Never enough. Always scraping by." All increase and decrease comes through words, and their words are bringing decrease! Money is not their problem. Their problem is their mouth. I tell them, "You can be broke, busted, and disgusted, but if you start speaking the Word of God instead of all that talk about never having enough and never getting ahead, things will start opening up for you. Doors of opportunity will come. Wisdom will come. Self-control will come. And you will see a change in your finances." Now don't get me wrong! There should be good stewardship and putting some feet to your faith, but a change in your life always begins with a change in your words.

The Church has been no better than the world in this area of confessing what they believe. There is very little faith, and often I find believers don't even know how faith works. They have to see it before they say it or believe it. They either haven't had a spiritual education or they refuse to walk in the truth they have been taught: In the kingdom of God you can't see it before you say it; you say it first and then you see it manifest. You bring it from the spirit realm into the natural realm with your words of faith.

Acting like God means first speaking like God. When you do that, you are being transformed inside out. However, when you speak all that loose, unbelieving talk, you are being conformed to the world's ways and thinking. If what I'm saying is hitting you right where you live, it's time you start calling "things which be not as though they were" (Romans 4:17). Then you are going to see miraculous results, just like Abraham and Sarah did.

Abraham and Sarah

Abram was ninety-nine years old and past the age of having kids. His body had stopped producing. His wife, Sarai, was ninety years old and had never been able to have children. Yet in Genesis 15:5, God had promised Abram that his descendants would be like the stars in the sky and that Sarai would give birth to their heir. In order for that to happen, God had to teach them about the law of confession.

> And when Abram was ninety years old and nine, the LORD appeared to Abram, and said unto him, I am the Almighty God; walk before me, and be thou perfect.
>
> And I will make my covenant between me and thee, and will multiply thee exceedingly.
>
> And Abram fell on his face: and God talked with him, saying,
>
> As for me, behold, my covenant is with thee, and thou shalt be a father of many nations.
>
> Neither shall thy name any more be called Abram, but thy name shall be Abraham; for a father of many nations have I made thee.
>
> Genesis 17:1-5

To fulfill the destiny He had planned for them, God waited until it was impossible in the natural for Abram and Sarai to have children before He acted. And then what did He do? He changed their names. In the passage of Scripture above, we read where God told Abram that his new name would be Abraham, which literally means "father of a multitude."[4]

> And God said unto Abraham, As for Sarai thy wife, thou shalt not call her name Sarai, but Sarah shall her name be.

And I will bless her, and give thee a son also of her: yea, I will bless her, and she shall be a mother of nations; kings of people shall be of her.

Then Abraham fell upon his face, and laughed, and said in his heart, Shall a child be born unto him that is an hundred years old? and shall Sarah, that is ninety years old, bear?

Genesis 17:15-17

God also changed Sarai's name to Sarah, and this name change was just as significant. The name Sarai had the connotation of a person who is domineering and contentious,[5] but the name Sarah referred to a "noble lady..., especially of the wives of a king of noble birth..., not concubines; a queen;.... This term was always used of royal women of the court."[6]

Think about this for a minute. God had not only given Abraham and Sarah new names, He had given them new identities—identities that they may not have been really comfortable with. Now everywhere they went, they had to tell all their friends and neighbors their new names. "Hi, I'm Abraham, you know, father of a multitude." People must have looked at his shriveled up old body and thought he was crazy.

Sarah was also going through a transformation as she spoke about herself in this new way. Taking on an identity of respect and honor meant she had to honor and respect her husband. No more trying to run the show and telling him what to do. No more nagging and fighting him on every whim. Don't you know, that must have begun to bring a warmth and youthfulness into her life. We can see this when the Lord came to visit Abraham one day.

And he said, I will certainly return unto thee according to the time of life; and, lo, Sarah thy wife shall have a son. And Sarah heard it in the tent door, which was behind him.

Now Abraham and Sarah were old and well stricken in age; and it ceased to be with Sarah after the manner of women.

Therefore Sarah laughed within herself, saying, After I am waxed old shall I have pleasure, my lord being old also?

And the LORD said unto Abraham, Wherefore did Sarah laugh, saying, Shall I of a surety bear a child, which am old?

Is any thing too hard for the LORD? At the time appointed I will return unto thee, according to the time of life, and Sarah shall have a son.

Then Sarah denied, saying, I laughed not; for she was afraid. And he said, Nay; but thou didst laugh.

Genesis 18:10-15

These verses show how Sarah was changing. She giggled like a schoolgirl at the idea of her and Abraham being sexually intimate and having a child, but the Lord asked her, "Is any thing too hard for the Lord?"

Abraham and Sarah started to call themselves what God had said about them. As they and all the people around them called them by their new names, the meanings of those names got down into their spirits. They began to see themselves as God saw them. Their confession affected them so much that it totally changed their physical bodies. In just three months Sarah conceived, and one year after her name was changed she gave birth to Isaac, the child God had promised.

Call It Like It Really Is

Therefore it is of faith, that it might be by grace; to the end the promise might be sure to all the seed; not to that only which is of the law, but to that also which is of the faith of Abraham; who is the father of us all,

(As it is written, I have made thee a father of many nations,) before him whom he believed, even God, who quickeneth the dead, and calleth those things which be not as though they were.

Romans 4:16-17

Did you know Abraham was your father? He is your father in the faith, and that means you can receive miracles from God the same way he did. Abraham acted like God, Who "calleth those things which be not as though they were." Every time Abraham and Sarah said their names they were calling things that were not as though they were. But in the spirit they were real! Their confession of faith was bringing what existed in the spirit into the natural world.

Who against hope believed in hope, that he might become the father of many nations, according to that which was spoken, So shall thy seed be.

And being not weak in faith, he considered not his own body now dead, when he was about an hundred years old, neither yet the deadness of Sarah's womb:

He staggered not at the promise of God through unbelief; but was strong in faith, giving glory to God;

And being fully persuaded that, what he had promised, he was able also to perform.

Romans 4:18-21

Verse 21 says they were "fully persuaded" that what God had promised was as good as done. They knew that if God had said it, it was real. What He had promised was already theirs. Now all they had to do was praise and thank Him for it.

When you know from God's Word that something is yours, believe it and call it like it really is—because it is! If God said it, then it is yours. It exists in the spirit realm and you bring it into the natural realm with your confession of faith. Acting like God means calling those things that are not as though they were—and they will be.

What Do You Call Yourself?

You have to stop calling yourself what the world and those around you call you—particularly the mean, hurtful things you may have been hearing for years—and start speaking what God says about you in His Word. He says you are His beloved and fully accepted (Ephesians 1:6). You are healed by the stripes Jesus bore on His back for you (1 Peter 2:24). All things pertaining to life and godliness are yours (2 Peter 1:3). You have all the wisdom of God in Christ Jesus (1 Corinthians 1:30).

When you begin to change the way you talk about yourself, some of your friends and family—and even some of your brothers and sisters in the Lord—may not understand. They may even think you've gone crazy or become arrogant. But this is part of what you signed up for when you took up your cross to follow Jesus. He had to deal with what His family and friends thought about Him because He told them who He was and did not conform to the world as they saw it.

> And when his friends heard of it, they went out to lay hold on him: for they said, He is beside himself.
>
> Mark 3:21

At one point in His ministry on Earth, Jesus' friends actually tried to physically remove Him because they thought He was "beside himself." These friends probably grew up with Jesus. They always thought He was a nice guy, although a little intense about religious stuff at times. But at this point, they thought He had gone too far and was acting insane. He had actually ordained twelve of His disciples to preach, cast out demons, and heal the sick (Mark 3:14-15). They were sure He was starting a dangerous cult!

Jesus also defined His family according to God's Word, which probably didn't go over too well either.

> There came then his brethren and his mother, and, standing without, sent unto him, calling him.
>
> And the multitude sat about him, and they said unto him, Behold, thy mother and thy brethren without seek for thee.
>
> And he answered them, saying, Who is my mother, or my brethren?
>
> And he looked round about on them which sat about him, and said, Behold my mother and my brethren!
>
> For whosoever shall do the will of God, the same is my brother, and my sister, and mother.
>
> Mark 3:31-35

Jesus also had to deal with the people of Nazareth, who had watched Him grow up.

> And when the sabbath day was come, he began to teach in the synagogue: and many hearing him were astonished, saying, From whence hath this man these things? and what wisdom is this which is given unto him, that even such mighty works are wrought by his hands?
>
> Is not this the carpenter, the son of Mary, the brother of James, and Joses, and of Juda, and Simon? and are not his sisters here with us? And they were offended at him.
>
> Mark 6:2-3

Speaking God's Word over yourself may lose you some friends and cause some misunderstanding in your family, but it will transform you from the inside out, just as it did Sarah and Abraham. God's truth will take root in your heart and change your image of who you are and what you are capable of accomplishing. You will become all God created you to be and do all He created you to do—and that is a powerful witness to all those friends and family members who thought you were crazy!

Acting like God in a world that hates God is not easy, but ultimately it will bring blessing and success into your life. Why? Because you will have what you say when you believe and say what God says.

8

Your Word Environment

Obviously, if your words control your life and you speak from whatever is in your heart, you need to watch what you are putting into your heart. What you hear and see are seeds planted into the soil of your heart, and a large part of what you experience is with friends and family. If you are going to live according to God's law of confession, you have to take a look at the folks you've been hanging around with. Think about what they talk about, because what you hear from them over and over again is going to get into your heart and shape your speech.

Relationships Plant Seed in Your Heart

Sometimes we are in a comfort zone with friends and family because they are familiar. We know them well and know what to expect. We think we can be ourselves with them—but what self is that? Are we acting like the child of God we are or like the person we were before we got saved? We may be in a comfort zone, but is it a comfort to our old, carnal nature and flesh? Is who we are with them and how we talk with them pleasing our flesh or God? Do the things we say line up with Scripture?

When I was in a fraternity, I spent most of my time around people who looked like me. In those days, that was important. But what matters now is being with people who talk like me, who are speaking and believing the Word of God over their lives. I certainly don't talk the way I used to. I used to say, "Every year at this time I catch the flu." I thought I was being truthful, based on past experience, but I wasn't speaking God's truth to change my future. This is what I learned to say,

> Because thou hast made the LORD, which is my refuge, even the most High, thy habitation;
> There shall no evil befall thee, neither shall any plague come nigh thy dwelling.
>
> Psalm 91:9-10

No plague shall come near me because I'm not who I used to be. I'm a new creation in Christ Jesus. The old things are passed away. If anything is not lining up with God's Word, I don't want it. And this new life sometimes means I have to hold old friends at arms length and make new friends who are walking the same path I'm walking.

You can't run with the rabbits and hunt with the hounds. You have to be either a hound or a rabbit. You can't run with people because they are the same color, the same profession, the same class, the same education, the same neighborhood, or even the same family. You run with those who are running with the truth.

You may have to stop spending a lot of time with some people if you're going to fulfill all that God has for your life. Remember—you are the only one who can stop you from fulfilling your destiny.

> No weapon that is formed against thee shall prosper; and every tongue that shall rise against thee in judgment thou shalt condemn. This is the heritage of the servants of the LORD, and their righteousness is of me, saith the LORD.
>
> Isaiah 54:17

According to this verse of Scripture, absolutely nothing can prevail against what God has for you in this life. This is your inheritance as a child of God. However, you have already read countless other verses that tell you how you can be defeated—and they all have to do with you and your words. Here are just a couple:

> He that keepeth his mouth keepeth his life: but he that openeth wide his lips shall have destruction.
>
> Proverbs 13:3

> Death and life are in the power of the tongue: and they that love it shall eat the fruit thereof.
>
> Proverbs 18:21

The only thing that can hinder or prevent you from prospering as God wants you to prosper in this life is your own mouth. You will eat the fruit of your lips, so you want to be speaking good things!

To speak as you desire to speak as a child of God, you need to hang out with other believers who understand these truths and can provoke you "unto love and good works" (Hebrews 10:24). You need to spend time with people who will plant the good seed of God's Word in your heart. Then you will continue to grow in faith and your confession will become more and more powerful and life-changing.

Bad Leadership Can Be Fatal

It's not just your friends and relatives who can get you to talking wrong. The leaders you listen to can do that too. This is what happened when Moses sent out the twelve spies to check out the land of Canaan. Those men were picked because they were the leaders of their tribes. They should have been the best and the brightest, but ten of the twelve came back with what God called an evil report.

> And they returned from searching of the land after forty days.
>
> And they went and came to Moses, and to Aaron, and to all the congregation of the children of Israel, unto the wilderness of Paran, to Kadesh; and brought back word unto them, and unto all the congregation, and shewed them the fruit of the land.
>
> And they told him, and said, We came unto the land whither thou sentest us, and surely it floweth with milk and honey; and this is the fruit of it.

Nevertheless the people be strong that dwell in the land, and the cities are walled, and very great: and moreover we saw the children of Anak there.

The Amalekites dwell in the land of the south: and the Hittites, and the Jebusites, and the Amorites, dwell in the mountains: and the Canaanites dwell by the sea, and by the coast of Jordan.

And Caleb stilled the people before Moses, and said, Let us go up at once, and possess it; for we are well able to overcome it.

But the men that went up with him said, We be not able to go up against the people; for they are stronger than we.

And they brought up an evil report of the land which they had searched unto the children of Israel, saying, The land, through which we have gone to search it, is a land that eateth up the inhabitants thereof; and all the people that we saw in it are men of a great stature.

And there we saw the giants, the sons of Anak, which come of the giants: and we were in our own sight as grasshoppers, and so we were in their sight.

Numbers 13:25-33

The twelve spies were the authority figures the rest of the Israelites looked to for leadership. The people hadn't been to Canaan or seen what it was like, so they relied on their leaders to give them a report. The report of the ten spies, which was the majority, did not line up with what God had said. He had said the land was already theirs, but they said they couldn't take it. In fact, they took God completely out of the situation because they compared themselves to the giants instead of comparing the giants to God. That's why the Bible called it an evil report.

Bad leaders usually sound reasonable on an intellectual level, but they always leave out God and what He says. Good leaders look at the facts and the information available to them, but then they always put God over any situation or problem. Then they say what He says and do what He tells them to do. Joshua and Caleb saw the same things the other ten spies saw, but they believed what God had said and put Him right in the center of their problem. Because they believed God was greater, their response to the giants and fortifications was that they were well able to take the land.

Joshua and Caleb were living proof that everyone rises or falls to the level of their confession. Forty years later, after those who had said they couldn't take the land had died in the wilderness, Joshua and Caleb were with those who took Canaan. They received what they had said they would receive, just as God had promised.

The devil didn't want the children of Israel back in Canaan and the government of Canaan didn't want them in there, but it made no difference. God had to honor what these men had spoken in faith. He had to honor their faith confession of His promise. No one could prevent Joshua and Caleb from achieving their destiny—and no one could prevent those who believed the evil report from having what they said either.

What the ten spies' perception did to the rest of the Israelites is recorded in Numbers 14:1-4.

> And all the congregation lifted up their voice, and cried; and the people wept that night.

And all the children of Israel murmured against Moses and against Aaron: and the whole congregation said unto them, Would God that we had died in the land of Egypt! or would God we had died in this wilderness!

And wherefore hath the LORD brought us unto this land, to fall by the sword, that our wives and our children should be a prey? were it not better for us to return into Egypt?

And they said one to another, Let us make a captain, and let us return into Egypt.

Ten leaders led millions of people astray and delayed God's plan for re-establishing Israel in the Promised Land for forty years. God was angry with all of them and said that none of those above twenty years old, except for Joshua and Caleb, would be allowed to enter Canaan (Numbers 14:29). These leaders cancelled out God's plan for many who died in the wilderness, and they postponed God's plan for the rest. They did all this with their words.

The ten spies allowed their circumstances and their perceptions—that the giants were too strong for them to overcome; that they themselves were only "grasshoppers"—to form their reality, instead of allowing the Word of God to form their reality. They spoke what they had heard and what they perceived. The people then spoke the same doubt and unbelief, and their words proved fatal for a whole generation of God's people.

There is one more thing I would like to add in light of the world you live in today. You cannot accept as the truth everything today's authority figures say. I know this will stir up some folks who read this, but it has to be said: Some leaders are very popular with the media and get very positive coverage, but what they are saying just isn't true. Unfortunately, lots of people look at these leaders and believe them, especially if they are the same color. You may not want to hear that, but that's one of the main reasons I was raised up—to confront these issues. My job is to promote God's truth over personalities and skin color, to confront contemporary culture with the culture of the kingdom of God, and to make sure God's people aren't deceived.

How Perceptions Differ

Perceptions are extremely important. All of us perceive things that, over time, drop down into our hearts until we come to believe them. When a couple comes to my office for counseling, they will talk about the same situation or event from completely different angles. They both experienced the same event, but they perceived what happened differently. It's the old "he said, she said" factor. And what they perceived determined how they acted and what they spoke.

Those perceptions became the trees that were rooted on the inside of them. Each was certain they were 100 percent correct in their assessment of the situation, and especially of the other person's thoughts, intentions, and behavior. Neither one could see the forest for the trees. Their perceptions (their trees) were formed by carnal, instead of godly, thinking and they could not see the big picture (the forest) because their own issues were in the way. As a counselor, I have to lead them to see those trees and uproot them. When their individual issues are dealt with, they can see each other and their situation from God's perspective and correct what needs to be corrected.

When you are dealing with a lot of different opinions and perspectives, the key is to get God's perspective. Think of the Israelites and remember that the majority is not always right. Don't ever let what the majority is thinking or saying influence you to go against the Word of God, or you may end up in the wilderness for forty years and never get to your promised land!

Perception is firmly rooted in your senses, and the enemy knows this. The ten spies based their report on their five senses—what they could see, touch, hear, taste or smell. That's how the devil wants you to operate, because he can only operate in the sense realm. He can always bring out something that will impress your senses in a way that intimidates you. He wants to sow misperceptions into your life, so that you won't fulfill the destiny God has planned for you.

Satan's goal is to get you to make decisions out of your soul, from your mind, emotions, and senses. He doesn't want you to be led by the Spirit and the Word in your spirit. Instead of having your mind renewed with God's Word, he will try to fill it with worldly reasoning and sense knowledge. When you allow that to happen, your carnal reasoning takes over and decides what is right and acceptable. Before long, that reasoning will drop down into your heart and grow, until without realizing it, what you are thinking, saying, and doing are totally against the Word of God.

None of us are smart enough on our own to out-reason the devil, but once we realize he's trying to pull something on us, all we have to do is tell him to get out. We don't have to yell and scream at him. Just get rid of him, and then begin to reject what our senses and carnal reasoning have been telling us. We must repent of all that and turn again to God's Word and the Holy Spirit for truth and wisdom.

As you hear and meditate the Word, you'll begin to get a fresh, new perception of your life and the situations you are facing. The Holy Spirit will give you revelation of things you have never seen before. The Word will illuminate your mind and spirit, and how you see everything will change for the better.

> Then said Jesus to those Jews which believed on him, If ye continue in my word, then are ye my disciples indeed;
>
> And ye shall know the truth, and the truth shall make you free.
>
> John 8:31-32

I hear a lot of believers talking about the truth setting them free, but they are not free. Why? They aren't continuing in the Word of God. To really become deception-proof in today's world, we must abide continually in God's Word. Only His truth will make us free and keep us free. Only the Word will keep us on the right path.

You Hear and Perceive Your Own Words

Do you know that when you hear yourself say something it has a huge impact on your own mind and heart? God knows this and the devil knows this, which is why they both want you to speak words that agree with their plan for your life. If you speak the devil's words, you will get the devil's plan. If you speak God's Word, you will get God's plan.

What you say affects other people, and it affects you.

> Whosoever therefore shall confess me before men, him will I confess also before my Father which is in heaven.
>
> But whosoever shall deny me before men, him will I also deny before my Father which is in heaven.
>
> Matthew 10:32-33

When you confessed Jesus as your Lord and Savior, that had an eternal and profound impact on you. But it doesn't stop there. Jesus wasn't talking only about getting saved; He was also talking about confessing His Word. Remember, He is the Truth (John 14:6) and the Word made flesh (John 1:14). When you confess what the Word says about your situation and your life, you are continuing to confess Him "before men."

> Nevertheless among the chief rulers also many believed on him; but because of the Pharisees they did not confess him, lest they should be put out of the synagogue:
>
> For they loved the praise of men more than the praise of God.
>
> John 12:42-43

The leaders of the synagogue were not worshipping in spirit and in truth because they never confessed Jesus as Lord, nor did they confess His Word. Some of the saddest words in the Bible are, "For they loved the praise of men more than the praise of God."

You cannot stay in an atmosphere that is based on dead religion and unbelief—in a church that confesses unbelief in God's Word—and not be affected by it. Soon you will be speaking what they are speaking. You will care more about what people think about you than what God thinks about you. Why does this happen? Words carry either spiritual life or spiritual death. They are more than sound. If God's Word spoken out of your own mouth brings you abundant life, what happens when you hear yourself say words of doubt and unbelief?

You may have heard believers say that if you hear a preacher say things that don't agree with the Word, you just spit out the sticks and chew on the hay that's good. That brings to mind the true story about a man and his mule. The mule wouldn't eat. His owner couldn't figure out what was wrong, so he called the veterinarian because the mule was getting weak. When the vet examined the mule, he found a stick stuck in his throat. So the vet just reached down the mule's throat, pulled out the stick, and the mule instantly started eating and was soon as good as ever.

I think the devil really likes that one about eating the hay and spitting out the sticks because he knows that one day, a stick could get lodged in your throat and cause some serious damage. That's why Jesus said in Mark 4:24, "Take heed what ye hear." What you hear can be hazardous to your faith. There are even things on Christian television that I won't watch.

Rest assured, the Holy Spirit inside you will tell you if you shouldn't listen to someone or something. But if you listen anyway, I can tell you what will happen. Initially you will hear some things you don't like or agree with, and you will begin talking about those things. The more you talk about them, the deeper they are planted in your heart. Then all the devil has to do is throw you some circumstances that will pull that very garbage out of your heart and right through your mouth. Before you know it, you are confessing the opposite of what God's Word says.

A more appropriate response is the moment you hear something that goes crossways with the Word, turn that preacher off, put down that book, throw away that CD—and open your Bible. Fill your heart and mind with the truth and begin confessing it out loud to yourself. When you hear the Word from your own lips, it is so easy to receive it because you were created to believe what you say. It can only produce good fruit in your life.

I'm not talking about walking in fear toward anything or anyone—only God. This is no different than being careful not to eat something that will make you sick or poison you and being diligent to eat the foods and drink the liquids that will make your body healthy and strong. Again, we see how the natural reflects the spiritual.

What you hear is going to affect and color what you perceive. What your parents, teachers, Sunday school teachers, and friends told you as a child—what you heard them say—still colors your perceptions today. This means that what you hear today will affect and color your perceptions tomorrow, and that is good news! You can change your life and receive all God has for you by simply changing what you hear, particularly what you hear yourself confessing. Then, instead of seeing everything through your "issues," you will perceive everything through God's eyes.

9

Reacting Right

The devil is not the only one who can sneak up on us and present us with something we never would have imagined. God has a way of throwing unexpected situations at us too. No matter what comes our way, if we understand the law of confession and trust in God and in His Word, we can take surprises in stride and give Him the opportunity to promote us and do awesome miracles.

In the New Testament, the angel Gabriel visited both Zacharias, John the Baptist's father, and Mary, the mother of Jesus. Each of them responded to his visit in an entirely different way.

Someone Who Missed It

Zacharias and his wife, Elisabeth, had been praying for a child for years without receiving their breakthrough.

There was in the days of Herod, the king of Judaea, a certain priest named Zacharias, of the course of Abia: and his wife was of the daughters of Aaron, and her name was Elisabeth.

And they were both righteous before God, walking in all the commandments and ordinances of the Lord blameless.

And they had no child, because that Elisabeth was barren, and they both were now well stricken in years.

Luke 1:5-7

Like Abraham and Sarah, Zacharias and Elisabeth were too old to have children. Also like Abraham and Sarah, God had a miracle baby for them. Gabriel visited Zacharias to give him the good news while he was doing his priestly duty in the temple.

And there appeared unto him an angel of the Lord standing on the right side of the altar of incense.

And when Zacharias saw him, he was troubled, and fear fell upon him.

But the angel said unto him, Fear not, Zacharias: for thy prayer is heard; and thy wife Elisabeth shall bear thee a son, and thou shalt call his name John.

And thou shalt have joy and gladness; and many shall rejoice at his birth.

For he shall be great in the sight of the Lord, and shall drink neither wine nor strong drink; and he shall be filled with the Holy Ghost, even from his mother's womb.

And many of the children of Israel shall he turn to the Lord their God.

And he shall go before him in the spirit and power of Elias, to turn the hearts of the fathers to the children, and the disobedient to the wisdom of the just; to make ready a people prepared for the Lord.

Luke 1:11-17

Gabriel told Zacharias that the child he and Elisabeth would have would be a great man of God and bring many people to the Lord. Zacharias responded by asking Gabriel to show him a sign to prove that what he was saying was true. The following verse shows us that Zacharias had more faith in his natural circumstances than in the word of the Lord.

And Zacharias said unto the angel, Whereby shall I know this? for I am an old man, and my wife well stricken in years.

Luke 1:18

The angel gave him a sign all right. Because he hadn't believed, Gabriel struck Zacharias dumb.

And the angel answering said unto him, I am Gabriel, that stand in the presence of God; and am sent to speak unto thee, and to shew thee these glad tidings.

And, behold, thou shalt be dumb, and not able to speak, until the day that these things shall be performed, because thou believest not my words, which shall be fulfilled in their season.

And the people waited for Zacharias, and marvelled that he tarried so long in the temple.

And when he came out, he could not speak unto them: and they perceived that he had seen a vision in the temple: for he beckoned unto them, and remained speechless.

Luke 1:19-22

Gabriel called his word from the Lord "glad tidings," but Zacharias was far from glad because he had no faith. Faith makes people glad. Obviously, Zacharias had not been planting God's Word in his heart and preparing himself to respond in faith to whatever God had for him. As a result, he responded with doubt and unbelief, and God couldn't take a chance that he would open his big mouth to either prevent the pregnancy or the birth of John. Therefore, He directed Gabriel to make Zacharias dumb, and he was unable to speak until John was born.

Someone Who Didn't Miss It

And in the sixth month the angel Gabriel was sent from God unto a city of Galilee, named Nazareth,

To a virgin espoused to a man whose name was Joseph, of the house of David; and the virgin's name was Mary.

And the angel came in unto her, and said, Hail, thou that art highly favoured, the Lord is with thee: blessed art thou among women.

And when she saw him, she was troubled at his saying, and cast in her mind what manner of salutation this should be.

And the angel said unto her, Fear not, Mary: for thou hast found favour with God.

Luke 1:26-30

Like Zacharias, Mary was afraid when Gabriel appeared. She also was "troubled at his saying" and wondered what it meant. She didn't doubt that God could do whatever He wanted to do, but she wanted to know how He was going to do it.

> And, behold, thou shalt conceive in thy womb, and bring forth a son, and shalt call his name JESUS.
>
> He shall be great, and shall be called the Son of the Highest: and the Lord God shall give unto him the throne of his father David:
>
> And he shall reign over the house of Jacob for ever; and of his kingdom there shall be no end.
>
> Then said Mary unto the angel, How shall this be, seeing I know not a man?
>
> And the angel answered and said unto her, The Holy Ghost shall come upon thee, and the power of the Highest shall overshadow thee: therefore also that holy thing which shall be born of thee shall be called the Son of God.
>
> Luke 1:31-35

Mary asked questions that were based upon her faith in God and His Word, not any unbelief. She quickly got with the plan of God.

> And Mary said, Behold the handmaid of the Lord; be it unto me according to thy word. And the angel departed from her.
>
> Luke 1:38

Mary's response to Gabriel was the right response. The words she spoke were in total agreement with God's Word. But just in case you are thinking you've already blown it too many times, let's go back and see what happened to Zacharias.

What If You've Missed It?

By the time John was born, Zacharias' faith in God's Word was high! He had obviously been spending time preparing his heart so he would respond only with God's Word no matter what happened. When the people were disputing Elisabeth's decision to call their son John, Zacharias wrote on a tablet, "His name is John" (Luke 1:63). He affirmed what the angel Gabriel had told him, and at that moment his tongue was loosed.

The first thing out of Zacharias' mouth was praise to God. He was finally rejoicing in the glad tidings Gabriel had spoken to him! Then he astonished everyone as God used him to prophesy about his newborn son and the soon-coming Messiah.

> And his father Zacharias was filled with the Holy Ghost, and prophesied, saying,
>
> Blessed be the Lord God of Israel; for he hath visited and redeemed his people,
>
> And hath raised up an horn of salvation for us in the house of his servant David;
>
> As he spake by the mouth of his holy prophets, which have been since the world began:
>
> That we should be saved from our enemies, and from the hand of all that hate us;
>
> To perform the mercy promised to our fathers, and to remember his holy covenant;
>
> The oath which he sware to our father Abraham,
>
> That he would grant unto us, that we being delivered out of the hand of our enemies might serve him without fear,

In holiness and righteousness before him, all the days of our life.

And thou, child, shalt be called the prophet of the Highest: for thou shalt go before the face of the Lord to prepare his ways;

To give knowledge of salvation unto his people by the remission of their sins,

Through the tender mercy of our God; whereby the dayspring from on high hath visited us,

To give light to them that sit in darkness and in the shadow of death, to guide our feet into the way of peace.

Luke 1:67-79

Zacharias may have blown it when Gabriel visited him, but he didn't wallow around in self-pity and condemnation. No, even though he couldn't talk, he determined that from that moment on that his words were going to line up with what God said and not what he thought. God knew his heart, and the moment he wrote, "His name is John," on that tablet, He set him free to speak again and used him to prophesy.

As you learn to operate in the law of confession, sometimes you might respond in unbelief like Zacharias did and sometimes you're going to respond in faith like Mary did. Either way, God is not through with you! If you miss it, don't crawl into a hole and put yourself in bondage over it. Just repent, get back in the Word, and move ahead with God.

On the other hand, if you don't miss it and respond in faith, don't think you've arrived! Stay humble and teachable. You still have a lot to learn and a destiny to fulfill. I've found through the years that when believers begin to operate in the law of confession and see great results, they can get arrogant and begin to take pride in what they are confessing and bringing to pass instead of being humbled by all God is doing in them, for them, and through them.

Proverbs 16:18 tells us, "Pride goeth before destruction, and an haughty spirit before a fall." So don't get into pride over your confession! Remind yourself that it is a privilege and an honor to be the vessel God is using to bring His kingdom to Earth, and it is His Word that is bringing that to pass. He should get all the glory.

Responding to the Impossible

Much of what God tells you either in His Word or by the Holy Spirit is going to be in the realm of the impossible, like a virgin conceiving, an elderly couple having a child, leading an entire nation out of slavery, or slaying a giant who has the entire world shaking in their shoes. But your job is to receive God's seed deep into your spirit and conceive what He tells you to conceive. Believe what He says and water that word with more of His Word and by praying in the Spirit.

God can't work through you except to the degree that you believe. You have to decide to let God be true and every man a liar (Romans 3:4). You can't do the impossible, but God can—and He calls upon you to decree it.

Thou shalt also decree a thing, and it shall be established unto thee.

Job 22:28

Decree in faith what God says, keep saying it and thanking Him for it, and God will do the rest. We find a perfect example of this if we go on with Mary's story. Other than the Lord's Prayer and Psalm 23, the following passage of Scripture is probably the most well-known. Most people call it, "The Christmas Story."

> And it came to pass in those days, that there went out a decree from Caesar Augustus that all the world should be taxed.
>
> (And this taxing was first made when Cyrenius was governor of Syria.)
>
> And all went to be taxed, every one into his own city.
>
> And Joseph also went up from Galilee, out of the city of Nazareth, into Judaea, unto the city of David, which is called Bethlehem; (because he was of the house and lineage of David:)
>
> To be taxed with Mary his espoused wife, being great with child.
>
> And so it was, that, while they were there, the days were accomplished that she should be delivered.
>
> And she brought forth her firstborn son, and wrapped him in swaddling clothes, and laid him in a manger; because there was no room for them in the inn.
>
> Luke 2:1-7

You are probably thinking, *Yeah, we read this every Christmas, but what does this have to do with the law of confession?* It has everything to do with it! In fact, it is a beautiful illustration of it. Back in the Old Testament, God spoke through the prophet Micah concerning where the Messiah would be born.

But thou, Bethlehem Ephratah, though thou be little among the thousands of Judah, yet out of thee shall he come forth unto me that is to be ruler in Israel; whose goings forth have been from of old, from everlasting.

Micah 5:2

Micah declared the word of the Lord that Jesus would be born in Bethlehem, but Mary and Joseph lived in Nazareth. Because God's Word never fails, Caesar Augustus had to declare taxation exactly when he did so Mary and Joseph would get to Bethlehem and the prophecy given hundreds of years earlier would be fulfilled. The prophet Micah had received this word from God, believed it and spoke it, and so it had to come to pass.

I could write an entire book on all the Old Testament prophecies that were miraculously fulfilled centuries later exactly as God said in His Word—and we are still seeing that today. Meditating on the 100 percent accuracy of Bible prophecy is one of the greatest faith builders for us when we want to give the right response to life's challenges and God's callings. Knowing what God is doing and continues to do using His people who operate in the law of confession, helps us to speak boldly and confidently when He calls on us to speak His Word.

An Early Lesson on the Right Response

My wife and I learned a great deal about the law of confession and how to respond right, which includes the need to keep quiet sometimes, when we were just starting out in the ministry in Chicago. We were amazed to see that we rose to the level of our confession.

We had been staying with a wonderful lady who opened up her home to us and our young son. We had been staying with her for eight months and I knew it was time for us to get out on our own, but every time we would get some money saved, a problem would come up. The car would break down or we would have another major expense we hadn't expected.

I said, "Wait a minute. Something's wrong here." I got before God, fasted for three days, and let Him talk to me. The first thing He said was, "Declare what you want." I knew we had no natural means to move and get out of that fine woman's home, so I turned to the supernatural ability of God and got out with my tongue.

I said, "All right. We'll be out of here in seven days." Now, nothing changed in the natural. We still didn't have the money or any other place to stay, but I told my wife, "Baby, we'll be out of here in seven days."

Naturally, she said, "Where are we going to go?"

I answered, "I don't know where we're going, but we'll be out of here in seven days."

The next day we were in the car and I said, "Well, six more days and we're going to be out of here." Now the pressure was on her to respond to this challenge to her faith. She had a great opportunity to open her mouth and say something that might have wrecked the whole thing, but she didn't. I watched her and she almost said something.

Tears came to her eyes, but she kept her mouth closed. I repeated, "We'll be out in six days."

The day after that, I got the idea we should be looking at places to rent. We still didn't have any money and nobody knew us, but we started looking, just driving around the city. Every place we drove by just didn't seem right for us, but then we drove by this nice, luxury apartment building. My son, who was still small and had been sleeping in the back seat, raised himself up, looked out the window, and said, "We're gonna live right there," and laid back down.

I wanted to smack him. I said, "Boy, close your mouth." But the Lord started working with my wife and me and told us we should go back over there. So we went in the building and asked the rental agent if we could look at some of the apartments for rent. We looked at a two-bedroom, a one-bedroom, and an efficiency. Then she said, "Okay, which one would you like?"

At that point in time I only had efficiency faith, so I said, "The efficiency."

She said, "Okay, we'll schedule this date to move your furniture in."

I looked at my wife and said, "Furniture?"

The lady said, "You don't have any furniture?"

We said, "Well, no, we gave it all away before we moved here."

She just said, "Oh, okay. We have some in the basement. It was the model apartment furniture. We'll let you use that." Then she said, "Let's see, that'll be one month's rent and one month's security."

I said, "Security?"

"You don't have the security?"

"No, ma'am."

"Well, all right. We'll just stretch your security out over one year and we'll let you pay that when you get it. Now, that'll be $55 to park in the underground parking."

I said, "Fifty-five dollars?"

She said, "Don't tell me. We'll turn on your electricity; we'll turn on your gas. We'll let you park."

God brought us right up to the level of our confession.

Not Out on a Limb

God wants to bless you so much—you just have to believe it and declare it! Declare the desires He has put in you and stand in faith for them. God likes it when you believe Him for big things and the impossible. Other people will try to bring your dreams down to the level where you can do it yourself. That's staying in the realm of the senses, where Satan can deceive you and destroy you and your dream. Don't go there! Let them think you are out on a limb having faith in God over your natural circumstances. You know that you are not out on a limb. You are standing on the rock of God's Word!

God wants you so far out in faith in Him that if He doesn't come through, you're really going to fail big. There is no limit for you except what you place on God. When you put your trust in Him, you have no limits. He is waiting on you to take a step beyond your own ability so He can get involved. His ears are itching to hear you declare His will and Word so that He can perform it.

> Then said the Lord to me, You have seen well, for I am alert and active, watching over My word to perform it.
>
> Jeremiah 1:12 AMP

We see well and respond well when we trust in God and His Word. One woman whose response to tragedy was legendary was the Shunammite woman in the Old Testament. She had been barren for years, but the prophet Elisha had declared she would have a son and she did. Then when the son was a young man working in the fields with his father, he fell ill and died (2 Kings 4:8-20). This is how his mother, the Shunammite woman, responded.

> And she went up, and laid him on the bed of the man of God, and shut the door upon him, and went out.
>
> And she called unto her husband, and said, Send me, I pray thee, one of the young men, and one of the asses, that I may run to the man of God, and come again.
>
> 2 Kings 4:21-22

Her first response was to go to the same man of God who had declared she would have a son. Her husband thought she was crazy. He said, "Where are you going? This ain't Sunday! This ain't mid-week service"(author's paraphrase).

Her second response was to her husband. She said, "It shall be well" (2 Kings 4:23). Then she rode out of town like a woman who wouldn't take no for an answer. When she arrived at Elisha's house, his servant Gehazi asked her how she was. Her third response was, "It is well" (2 Kings 4:26). This woman did not let death come out of her mouth! She only spoke life.

You can read the rest of the story in 2 Kings 4:27-37, but know that this woman got what she said. Elisha raised her son from the dead. All was well. It was well when she spoke it because she knew that God's promises were yes and amen (2 Corinthians 1:20). He had promised her a son. He had not promised her a son who would die prematurely. And so she spoke the truth that she believed in her heart, and she got what she said.

When you are faced with impossible situations or heart-wrenching tragedy, remember the saints who have gone before you. Build your faith by reading Hebrews 11 and meditating on those who overcame insurmountable odds with their confession of faith. Then speak only the truth of God's Word and refuse to budge until you see His promise manifest in your life.

10

Believing the Best

Part of what God called me to do is to teach His people that Jesus died to give them an inheritance, that He has a plan for their success and happiness. But first they must understand that whether He has them renting a room or living in a mansion, they are kings serving directly under *the King*. When a believer gets the revelation that they are a king who lives and moves and has their being in *the King*, they will remain humble while no longer settling for living far below the spiritual, mental, emotional, social, professional, and financial prosperity He has for them.

I said in the last chapter that we rise to the level of our confession, so my first challenge—in my own life and then with my congregation—has been to change what we say about ourselves. To change what we say about ourselves, we have to come to grips with what we believe about ourselves because we generally say what we believe. We need to get honest and compare what we really believe about ourselves with what God says about us in His Word. If what we believe does not line up with what God says, then we need to change what we believe and say only what He says about us.

We have talked about how sometimes we say things about ourselves that we don't really believe. This is not good because our hearts and mouths were created to be in agreement. The power of our words comes from the agreement between what we believe in our hearts and speak with our mouths.

This is why the devil doesn't want us to practice this revelation of the laws of confession and agreement: it brings God's power on the scene! When we speak what we believe and what we believe agrees with God, then we are one within and one with Him. The enemy knows he is powerless over this double-agreement.

Even John the Baptist and Jesus

And this is the record of John, when the Jews sent priests and Levites from Jerusalem to ask him, Who art thou?

And he confessed, and denied not; but confessed, I am not the Christ.

And they asked him, What then? Art thou Elias? And he saith, I am not. Art thou that prophet? And he answered, No.

Then said they unto him, Who art thou? that we may give an answer to them that sent us. What sayest thou of thyself?

He said, I am the voice of one crying in the wilderness, Make straight the way of the Lord, as said the prophet Esaias.

John 1:19–23

Where did John get all that information about himself? Where did he get all those beliefs? He got them from the Old Testament. The book of Isaiah revealed to John the Baptist the truth about who he was. Then he confessed who he was based on what the Word of God said, not what he had heard from his mother Elisabeth or from her cousin Mary—or from some bully down the street who called him names.

John was not the only person who found out who he was and what he believed from the Word of God.

And he came to Nazareth, where he had been brought up: and, as his custom was, he went into the synagogue on the sabbath day, and stood up for to read.

And there was delivered unto him the book of the prophet Esaias. And when he had opened the book, he found the place where it was written,

The Spirit of the Lord is upon me, because he hath anointed me to preach the gospel to the poor; he hath sent me to heal the brokenhearted, to preach deliverance to the captives, and recovering of sight to the blind, to set at liberty them that are bruised,

To preach the acceptable year of the Lord.

And he closed the book, and he gave it again to the minister, and sat down. And the eyes of all them that were in the synagogue were fastened on him.

And he began to say unto them, This day is this scripture fulfilled in your ears.

Luke 4:16-21

What was Jesus doing? He was confessing who He was. From the moment He could read, He had studied the Scriptures. He found out what God, His Father, said about Him. He didn't ask His parents or the Jewish leaders. He just took God's Word, believed what it said about Him, and then confessed what it said about Him.

Jesus told us to follow Him (John 10:27), and we are to be like Him in every way. So where are we to find our true identity? Where will we discover who we really are and what we were created to do in this life? The same place Jesus and John the Baptist found their identity: in the Bible. Only God's Word can tell us who we are and what is our purpose. Then, once we know who God says we are—once we get the revelation of being kings and priests unto our God (Revelation 5:10)—then we can begin to reign in life by saying what we believe about ourselves.

> For if by one man's offence death reigned by one; much more they which receive abundance of grace and of the gift of righteousness shall reign in life by one, Jesus Christ.
>
> Romans 5:17

Are you reigning in life or is life trampling you down before you get out of bed in the morning? If you are not reigning, then open up the Book and find out who you are. Then don't let anything come out of your mouth except what God says you are. Tell the real truth about yourself! You are a child of the Most High God. You have gifts to use and callings to fulfill.

This is very similar to when I'm flying an airplane. The air traffic controller will say to me, "Flight 020 Tango, turn right heading 320, maintain 5,000 feet. Roger." When he says, "Roger," he is asking me to confirm that I heard and agree with what he just told me to do.

I answer him, saying, "020 Tango (that's me) is turning, heading 320, maintaining 5,000 feet." If I don't say that, the controller will come back on the radio and say, "020 Tango, did you receive my transmission?" He won't let up until I say what he said. I have to say what he says because that is the air traffic control tower's way of keeping track of all the airplanes in their area. I'm safe because they keep me from running into any other airplane in their area. They do that by continually checking my position, correcting my path if necessary, and having me say what they said to confirm it.

The only way you are going to remain safe, secure, blessed, and able to be a blessing to everyone around you is to continue to say what your heavenly air traffic controller is saying to you, through you, and about you.

You are growing in the knowledge of Him, maturing in the faith, and becoming more and more like Jesus every day. That's who you are! And when you believe who you are and speak who you are, then you can buy that building, open that business, teach that class, get that degree, or launch that worldwide ministry. You can find the right mate, have a great marriage, raise up godly children and grand-children—and be rejoicing and flying high!

People Aren't Your Problem— Or Your Answer

Terrible things happen to believers who don't have any understanding of who they are in Christ and who speak unbelief and negative things about themselves. They don't think much of themselves and so end up comparing themselves to others, trying to find someone who looks smaller than them. Then they can feel better about themselves. Of course, if they find someone who looks bigger than they are, they have a rough time!

The children of Israel had no understanding of who they were as children of the Most High God when they heard both an evil report and a good report from the twelve spies. They saw themselves as small, and said, "We are like grasshoppers compared to those giants!" Giants were not their problem; their tongues were their problem and their tongues spoke what they believed. Thus, they never got to their wealthy place in God. They said they couldn't take the Promised Land and they didn't.

Today, too many of my brothers and sisters in the faith do the same thing. Their giant is "the man." That's who they blame for their problems. They blame whoever is the president or their boss or their neighborhood leader. They blame the white man or the black man or the red man. They blame the unions or the management. They blame everyone but themselves. The devil loves this! As long as they don't take responsibility for their own lives and continue talking the blame game, he can keep them running in circles with hatred, rage, bitterness, fear, frustration, and worse. Their own mouths are giving the devil permission to give them exactly what they are complaining about!

When we believe other people are our problem, what happens to us? We just get more and more frustrated, bitter, and angry. But the Bible says we are supposed to go into Canaan with joy. We draw water out of the wells of salvation with joy and we move toward our wealthy place in Christ Jesus with high-fives, slapping hands. "Praise God! I'm a king and priest unto God and He has given me this building! I am well able to take it."

If anyone believes another human being or group of human beings is their problem, they have been sold a bill of goods. That is not the truth. The truth is found in Romans 8:31, where God tells us that if He is for us no one can be against us. In other words, no human being or demonic power can stop us when we are walking with the Lord and our hearts believe and our mouths speak what He says about us.

My enemies can talk ugly about me as much as they want; as long as God is for me, no person can stand against me. I don't have to fight them with my hands. I don't have to go into training and have a confrontation. All I have to do is train my tongue and watch God overpower my enemies in bringing His Word to pass.

I fight with the sword of the Spirit that's coming out of my mouth. I don't have to win a few, lose a few. The Word of God says in 2 Corinthians 2:14, "Now thanks be unto God, which always causeth us to triumph in Christ." Because God is on my side, I'm going to win every time.

No other human being or evil spirit has any authority over my life unless I give them permission. None. God didn't give anyone the right to stop me. For a while, when we were believing and confessing that the mall was ours, I had wrong thinking in this area. God really jumped on me about it, so I had to change my thinking. He said, "Are you believing to buy this mall debt-free?"

I said, "Yes, Sir."

He said, "What are you doing about the people? Where do they come in?"

I said, "Well, I'm trusting in them."

God said, "Trusting in them? When you do that, they can stop you."

He was reminding me that the people weren't my source of supply in purchasing anything. He was, and He is a jealous God. He wants to be our only source because He knows that's the best thing for us. It's not jealousy like we know it. His jealousy is always motivated by love and the desire to bless. He knows we're not going to be blessed if we have our faith in anyone or anything but Him.

Do you see why people are not your problem or your answer? If you have a troublesome situation going on in your life—it can be something that just came out of nowhere or something you've been dealing with for years—then your problem has been what you've been believing and speaking. Your answer is found in God's Word and speaking the truth, fully trusting in God and God alone.

The Believing Crisis

Sometimes what you believe about yourself doesn't line up with the Word of God. That's when you find yourself in a believing crisis. It may be hard to believe what God is saying about you because everything and everyone in your past experience has told you the exact opposite. "You might as well face it. This world is never going to like your color or where you come from. There's no way you are getting out of this neighborhood. There's no money for education, so you best settle for what you've got."

Then you read in God's Word that you are His workmanship and should walk in the works He's prepared for you to walk in (Ephesians 2:10). You read that you can do all things through Jesus Christ, who strengthens you (Philippians 4:13). And one day you pick up your Bible, open it, and out jumps 2 Peter 1:3, "His divine power hath given unto us all things that pertain unto life and godliness."

Should you believe your past or what God's Word says?

For what if some did not believe? shall their unbelief make the faith of God without effect?

God forbid: yea, let God be true, but every man a liar; as it is written, That thou mightest be justified in thy sayings, and mightest overcome when thou art judged.

Romans 3:3-4

God speaks the truth, whether we believe it or not. Just because someone you know and have had great respect for in the past believes Jesus is not the only way to Heaven doesn't make that true. In fact, they are wrong. They may sincerely believe that they can get to Heaven another way, but they are always going to be wrong. Why? Because God is always right, and He says Jesus is the only way to Heaven.

The same principle applies to you. God is always right. It doesn't matter what is happening in your life now or what has been happening up until now. If it's not what He said, it isn't you and it isn't for you. Find the verse of Scripture you need for your situation, put it in your heart, and out of the abundance of the heart you will say the truth about yourself and your situation. If God can get your heart and mouth to change, your life will change.

Someone may be saying, "I just want to tell the truth." The Word of God is the truth. When you say it and keep on saying it, it gets down into your heart. Mark 11:23 says you can have doubt in your head but not in your heart. Your carnal mind may fight you on it, but your heart and mouth can still agree and defeat any thought of doubt or unbelief. When you practice this, you'll see that God will meet all your needs, and then you will be better able to meet the needs of others.

What you see in your life may be a fact, a condition at this moment in time. But the power of the truth of the Word to change that condition is the same as the power of light against darkness. In a dark room you don't have to run the darkness out; you just have to turn on the light. When you get serious about only speaking the truth, that lie that's confronting you—whether it's disease or lack or whatever—has to go. It's been exposed. When the doctor tells you there's nothing he can do, tell him, "Step aside. I'm about to speak to it."

When you are in a believing crisis, you have to choose to take God at His Word and forget what anybody else says or has said. You have to become convinced that God and His Word cannot lie. To grow in faith in the absolute truth of God's Word, go straight to His Word (Romans 10:17). Every word is a seed that is spirit and life and has unlimited potential.

You need to plant the seed of God's Word in every situation you face. You can't assume you have the internal image you need to meet the present challenges in your life just because you're a baptized, tongue-talking member of a Full Gospel church for forty years. What happens is, we think we have the image right, but we are always growing in the knowledge of Him (2 Peter 3:18). If we think we've arrived, our pride and ignorance give Satan a chance to con us and even use us.

A seed you might be able to use in a believing crisis is Titus 1:2.

> In hope of eternal life, which God, that cannot lie, promised before the world began.

This verse doesn't only say that God won't lie, it says He *cannot* lie. This means that whatever He says goes. If you think today is Sunday and God says it's Tuesday, you can forget about going to church service because the sanctuary doors will be locked. When God says it's Tuesday, it is Tuesday. What God says controls the universe. It's a done deal. Furthermore, what God says about you in His Word is also a done deal. He's just waiting for you to believe it and say it so you can have it.

Beware of Golden Calves

For my thoughts are not your thoughts, neither are your ways my ways, saith the LORD.

For as the heavens are higher than the earth, so are my ways higher than your ways, and my thoughts than your thoughts.

Isaiah 55:8-9

We have a hard time believing what God says about us because His thoughts and ways are so different from what we are used to. We have seen that when Moses stayed too long on the mountain talking to God—as far as the children of Israel were concerned—they built what was in their heart, what they were familiar with and comfortable with. They built a golden calf. That calf represented the religion of Egypt and their life of slavery. They didn't know anything different and they hadn't decided to believe and trust this powerful God of their forefathers who thundered on the mountain.

People bring all kinds of golden calves into our church from their old churches: how the choir sang, how they took the offering, the way they did Vacation Bible School. Then there are the sinners with their golden calves. We see the wealthy drug dealer who gets saved but doesn't want to give up their rich lifestyle to make an honest living. There is the woman who has been saved for years and has never dealt with the fact that she had an abortion. There is the young teenager who has been sexually and physically abused but loves Jesus with all their heart.

We love all these people, and God has plans to take every golden calf out of them. For many this removal will take major surgery. Their golden calf makes them believe they're right in breaking the law of the land, doing what they needed to do at the time, or being in a rage at everyone else because their life has been so painful—but they're wrong because none of this lines up with the Word of God.

I can speak boldly about this because everyone has golden calves, and I was no exception. I learned a great deal about how the law of confession can change your life when my wife and I were first married. I had come from a family that was divorced, struggling, and fighting all the time. All that was loaded into me. There was a tree of division and divorce in my heart that formed my perception of family life.

After we had been married four or five months and some of the thrill was gone, I began to complain and find fault with my wife. I didn't like how the roast was done, how she squeezed the toothpaste tube—little things like that. This was coming from the tree of fighting and fussing that was inside me. I began to think thoughts like, "God, this woman thou gavest me...," and "How can I get out of this?"

God knew what I needed. He sent me to a meeting where the preacher talked about calling things that be not as though they were. Afterwards, I found a little book at the book table called *Praying God's Word,* by Ed Dufresne. It said to pray out loud what you needed, according to the Word of God.

Well I wanted a perfect wife, so I found Proverbs 31 and began praying it out loud over my wife. Here are some of the verses I prayed over her.

> Strength and honour are her clothing; and she shall rejoice in time to come.
>
> She openeth her mouth with wisdom; and in her tongue is the law of kindness.
>
> She looketh well to the ways of her household, and eateth not the bread of idleness.
>
> Her children arise up, and call her blessed; her husband also, and he praiseth her.
>
> Many daughters have done virtuously, but thou excellest them all.
>
> Favour is deceitful, and beauty is vain: but a woman that feareth the LORD, she shall be praised.
>
> Give her of the fruit of her hands; and let her own works praise her in the gates.
>
> Proverbs 31:25-31

In the beginning my mind said, "None of that's true," as I rattled off these verses day after day. But it was the Word of God, and we know that the Word of God will stand true no matter what doubts our minds come up with. The more I heard my mouth say it and the more I planted that good seed in my heart, the more I became persuaded that that Proverbs 31 woman was my wife.

My heart and my mouth were in agreement with what God said about my wife and that was that. The turmoil I had in my early marriage was still a fact, but the truth of the Word changes facts. I kept saying what the Word said about my wife, and it was seed. I was planting new seed—spirit and life—into my heart.

So what happened? What I was confessing about my wife didn't change her; it changed me! The Word pulled out that old tree of division and divorce, the one I didn't know about that I had carried in me for years—from the house where I grew up in Tuskegee, Alabama, to Chicago, and on to Minneapolis, where we were right after we got married. What I had been praying and speaking for my wife had replaced that old tree. Now I had a new tree inside me that was producing all the right fruit. I began to see and love my Proverbs 31 woman in a whole new way—God's way!

Today we have a marriage made in Heaven. That's because the seed we used to make our marriage work came from Heaven. Back then, I would have told you that two people couldn't stay in the same home for a week without arguing. Now, I can't even remember the last time we had an argument. There is peace in our home. That kind of peace can be yours too—peace that passes all understanding. You just have to put the law of confession into practice.

What are the golden calves you have harbored in your life? You just have to immerse yourself in God's Word to expose them and replace the bondage and deception with truth. I can tell you from personal experience that you can't even imagine the joy and peace and success God has for you when you throw out that old, "stinkin' thinkin'" and begin believing and speaking what God says.

Be Fully Persuaded

Whatever you need, find the verses of Scripture that address that need. In my situation, I was having trouble with my wife so I found Proverbs 31 and other passages that talked about a godly wife and began to declare them over my wife. I made up my mind that seed was going deep into my heart. I believed it, and the truth that seed carried was the only thing that was coming out of my mouth. It wasn't long before I was fully persuaded that my wife was the godliest woman on the planet!

I believe the Church has been held back in every area of life because we say things that don't line up with God's Word and think we're being honest. God is trying to take us into our Promised Land and we are saying, "We can't afford it." Think about that. Where did that statement come from—and where did it go? It came from the devil and went right into our hearts. We say, "But I'm just being honest." We are being honest about our budget, but we are not speaking the truth about what we have available to us through Jesus Christ. The truth says God shall supply all our needs according to His riches in glory (Philippians 4:19).

When God tells you to go buy some land or build a building, He is not waiting for you to say, "I can't afford it." He is waiting for you to speak the world-changing, hindrance-removing, creative words that you can do all things through

Him (Philippians 4:13). You should meditate and confess those words until that image is so real in your heart that you cannot conceive of anything different.

When the Word goes into your heart, it begins to grow inside of you. Over time, you and that Word become one. You don't know where the Word stops and you start. That is being fully persuaded. You are going to prevail. You are coming back to the top. You are taking dominion over the fish of the sea, over the fowl of the air, over the money, over the disease, and over sin.

You have to make the commitment to stand on God's Word and keep saying it until it is so real in your heart you just can't say anything different. Say it until you fully believe it and are fully persuaded. Then when you speak it, God has to bring it to pass. And He's been waiting to bless you! In fact, He wanted to bless you so much that He sent Jesus to die for your sins so He could bless you. Knowing this, how can you not speak what He wants and what you want over your children, over your finances, over your Aunt Hattie to be healed from cancer, or over that cousin of yours to get saved?

> But what saith it? The word is nigh thee, even in thy mouth, and in thy heart: that is, the word of faith, which we preach;
>
> That if thou shalt confess with thy mouth the Lord Jesus, and shalt believe in thine heart that God hath raised him from the dead, thou shalt be saved.
>
> For with the heart man believeth unto righteousness; and with the mouth confession is made unto salvation.

For the scripture saith, Whosoever believeth on him shall not be ashamed.

For there is no difference between the Jew and the Greek: for the same Lord over all is rich unto all that call upon him.

Romans 10:8-12

This passage in Romans spells it all out for us. The Greek word translated salvation in verse 10 comes from the root word *sozo,* which simply means "to save," and is the word *soteria,* which means, "Deliverance, preservation, salvation. Used of material and temporal deliverance...; of spiritual and eternal deliverance...; of the present experience of God's power to deliver...; of the future deliverance at the ...Second Coming of Christ...; inclusively of all the blessing of God."[1]

This word covers everything you need now and forever: eternal salvation, deliverance, healing, prosperity, protection, soundness—all blessing. It's much more than just getting a ticket to Heaven when you die. It is a quality of life now, as well as then. Following this path of confession in Romans 10:10, you will succeed in every area of life. And verses 11 and 12 say you will not be ashamed and God will be rich unto you, no matter what color your skin is or where you came from or what you have experienced in your past.

Believing in your heart won't always come easily, but it's vital that you keep working on it because what you believe in your heart will determine who you are and what you are doing in your future. You will speak your destiny from what you believe in your heart. You may have enjoyed the fruit of practicing the law of confession in one area of your life, but now you are faced with a new challenge in another area. You know what to do! You need to begin planting the incorruptible seed of God's Word in your heart and become fully persuaded that what He says trumps any circumstance or lying words of the enemy.

Your challenge is not unlike that faced by the two blind men in Matthew 9:27-29.

> And when Jesus departed thence, two blind men followed him, crying, and saying, Thou son of David, have mercy on us.
>
> And when he was come into the house, the blind men came to him: and Jesus saith unto them, Believe ye that I am able to do this? They said unto him, Yea, Lord.
>
> Then touched he their eyes, saying, According to your faith be it unto you.

Jesus asked a hard question when He said, "Do you believe I can make your blind eyes see?" He was asking them, "Do you believe the impossible?" They said they believed, and Jesus said it would be done according to their faith. It was not because of their age, their education, their family lineage, their color, or their gifts and talents. It was because of their faith. They were fully persuaded, and that's why they received their sight.

Believing Has No Limits

Whatever you need, gather as many verses as you can about it. Put them on your wall, your refrigerator, in the car, and wherever you'll be continually reminded of the truth. Then begin to use the law of confession until the truth of God's Word completely overpowers the facts you are dealing with. Put the Word in your mouth and plant it in your heart, and out of the abundance of your heart you will produce an abundance of what you need. Don't leave this Earth with anything still on the table. Tell God, "Father, I want everything you've got for me. I want to be a show house for Your kingdom."

A sixteen-year-old boy in one of our services gave an amazing testimony. He said he had believed for and received a house that was fully paid for, which he gave to his mama. We asked if he knew that meant he had sowed that house as a seed. He said, "Yes, sir. I'm believing for a mansion now." That boy was thinking big, and God loves it when we think big. Now you understand why Jesus said we should all be as little children (Matthew 18:3-4)!

Don't put any limits on the amount and the ways in which God wants to bless you. Do not limit Him by believing things that have nothing to do with what He says in His Word, or by believing the facts more than God's truth. Right now you need to get honest with yourself about what you really believe and uproot any bad trees in your heart that go crosswise with the truth. Then you can believe God for all the outrageously impossible things He wants you to be and to do.

11

Triumph Even in Tough Times

One day we went into a car dealership to buy a car. As we walked in, a salesman with a big smile on his face said, "Pastor Winston!"

I said, "Yeah, un-huh." I didn't think I knew him.

He introduced himself and said, "I watch your program." He asked me what kind of car we wanted and I told him. On the way to look I said, "Well, how are sales going?"

He said, "Well it would be going much better if we had somebody different in the office."

I asked, "Oh, your boss not treating you quite right, huh?"

"Oh no, I'm not talking about that. I'm talking about the White House."

Notice what he did. He put his future in the hands of the White House. He blamed the president of the United States for his problems, for his lack of sales. It made me wonder if he had ever really heard what I was teaching on television!

When you're a Christian, nobody's to blame for your future but you. Why? Because a good man speaks good things out of the good deposits or treasures of his heart (Matthew 12:35). You have what you say. The truth is, that man could make all kinds of sales and be rolling in commissions if he would just change what he was confessing.

Furthermore, if anyone thinks that the government can stop them, they haven't read their Bible. In both the Old Testament and the New Testament there are many examples of how God's people prevailed over the civil rulers and governments of their time. One of my favorite examples is the account in the book of Daniel of three young Hebrew men who had been captured and taken to Babylon to serve a pagan king. Their story began when King Nebuchadnezzar decided to make a gold statue of himself.

> Nebuchadnezzar the king made an image of gold, whose height was threescore cubits, and the breadth thereof six cubits: he set it up in the plain of Dura, in the province of Babylon.
> Then Nebuchadnezzar the king sent to gather together the princes, the governors, and the captains, the judges, the treasurers, the counsellors, the sheriffs, and all the rulers of the provinces, to come to the dedication of the image which Nebuchadnezzar the king had set up.
> Then the princes, the governors, and captains, the judges, the treasurers, the counsellors, the sheriffs, and all the

rulers of the provinces, were gathered together unto the dedication of the image that Nebuchadnezzar the king had set up; and they stood before the image that Nebuchadnezzar had set up.

Then an herald cried aloud, To you it is commanded, O people, nations, and languages,

That at what time ye hear the sound of the cornet, flute, harp, sackbut, psaltery, dulcimer, and all kinds of musick, ye fall down and worship the golden image that Nebuchadnezzar the king hath set up:

And whoso falleth not down and worshippeth shall the same hour be cast into the midst of a burning fiery furnace.

Daniel 3:1-6

Shadrach, Meshach, and Abednego worked for the king and had great favor with him; but they had enemies in the court who were Chaldeans. They were jealous of these very gifted and talented young men who were devout Jews and refused to worship anyone but God.

Wherefore at that time certain Chaldeans came near, and accused the Jews.

They spake and said to the king Nebuchadnezzar, O king, live for ever.

Thou, O king, hast made a decree, that every man that shall hear the sound of the cornet, flute, harp, sackbut, psaltery, and dulcimer, and all kinds of musick, shall fall down and worship the golden image:

And whoso falleth not down and worshippeth, that he should be cast into the midst of a burning fiery furnace.

There are certain Jews whom thou hast set over the affairs of the province of Babylon, Shadrach, Meshach, and Abednego; these men, O king, have not regarded thee:

they serve not thy gods, nor worship the golden image which thou hast set up.

Then Nebuchadnezzar in his rage and fury commanded to bring Shadrach, Meshach, and Abednego. Then they brought these men before the king.

Nebuchadnezzar spake and said unto them, Is it true, O Shadrach, Meshach, and Abednego, do not ye serve my gods, nor worship the golden image which I have set up?

Daniel 3:8-14

This new law put these boys in a terrible bind. If they continued to defy the king and refused to bow to his statue, they would be thrown in a fiery furnace and burned to death. But they knew something their enemies didn't know. They were in the world but not of the world. They knew that spiritual laws ruled over natural laws—that their Creator reigned over His creation—even fiery furnaces.

Shadrach, Meshach, and Abednego, answered and said to the king, O Nebuchadnezzar, we are not careful to answer thee in this matter.

If it be so, our God whom we serve is able to deliver us from the burning fiery furnace, and he will deliver us out of thine hand, O king.

But if not, be it known unto thee, O king, that we will not serve thy gods, nor worship the golden image which thou hast set up.

Daniel 3:16-18

These boys had no hesitation in telling the king that their God was able to deliver them, but even if He didn't they would never bow down to anything or anyone but Him.

The king wasn't exactly thrilled with their confession of faith.

> Then was Nebuchadnezzar full of fury, and the form of his visage was changed against Shadrach, Meshach, and Abednego: therefore he spake, and commanded that they should heat the furnace one seven times more than it was wont to be heated.
>
> And he commanded the most mighty men that were in his army to bind Shadrach, Meshach, and Abednego, and to cast them into the burning fiery furnace.
>
> Then these men were bound in their coats, their hosen, and their hats, and their other garments, and were cast into the midst of the burning fiery furnace.
>
> Therefore because the king's commandment was urgent, and the furnace exceeding hot, the flames of the fire slew those men that took up Shadrach, Meshach, and Abednego.
>
> And these three men, Shadrach, Meshach, and Abednego, fell down bound into the midst of the burning fiery furnace.
>
> Daniel 3:19-23

In a rage, the king had Shadrach, Meshach, and Abednego bound and thrown into the fiery furnace, which he had commanded to be seven times hotter than usual. It was so hot that the big men who threw them in were burned to death! But the boys were without fear, for they believed their God—and He showed up beyond anyone's wildest dreams.

> Then Nebuchadnezzar the king was astonished, and rose up in haste, and spake, and said unto his counsellors, Did not we cast three men bound into the midst of the fire? They answered and said unto the king, True, O king.

He answered and said, Lo, I see four men loose, walking in the midst of the fire, and they have no hurt; and the form of the fourth is like the Son of God.

Daniel 3:24-25

What happened when Shadrach, Meshach, and Abednego spoke out of the abundance of their hearts? Jesus danced in the fire with them! God honored their confession of faith, and that awesome show of God's power completely humbled old King Nebuchadnezzar.

Then Nebuchadnezzar came near to the mouth of the burning fiery furnace, and spake, and said, Shadrach, Meshach, and Abednego, ye servants of the most high God, come forth, and come hither. Then Shadrach, Meshach, and Abednego, came forth of the midst of the fire.

And the princes, governors, and captains, and the king's counsellors, being gathered together, saw these men, upon whose bodies the fire had no power, nor was an hair of their head singed, neither were their coats changed, nor the smell of fire had passed on them.

Then Nebuchadnezzar spake, and said, Blessed be the God of Shadrach, Meshach, and Abednego, who hath sent his angel, and delivered his servants that trusted in him, and have changed the king's word, and yielded their bodies, that they might not serve nor worship any god, except their own God.

Therefore I make a decree, That every people, nation, and language, which speak any thing amiss against the God of Shadrach, Meshach, and Abednego, shall be cut in pieces, and their houses shall be made a dunghill: because there is no other God that can deliver after this sort.

Then the king promoted Shadrach, Meshach, and Abednego, in the province of Babylon.

Daniel 3:26-30

Shadrach, Meshach, and Abednego didn't even smell like smoke! The king was so impressed, he made a decree stating that no one could speak against the God of Shadrach, Meshach, and Abednego; and then he promoted them. Because of their confession of faith, the king had become a witness for the Most High God along with them.

Now I want you to consider this: Shadrach, Meshach, and Abednego were not born again or filled with the Spirit. They didn't have the New Testament to read about their authority in Jesus Christ. They didn't even know about Jesus Christ except as the Messiah to come. And yet their confession of faith in the God of Abraham produced an incredible miracle and changed the heart of a pagan king. With that in mind, what should we be doing in this world, since we are born-again, Holy Ghost filled, New Testament saints?

The Law of Confession
Overcomes Governments

Wherefore seeing we also are compassed about with so great a cloud of witnesses....

Hebrews 12:1

There are many saints of God who have gone before us and changed the world through their confession of faith and they are watching us from the grandstands of Heaven, cheering us on. Whenever we get weary or discouraged, all we need to do is open our Bibles and read about our brothers and sisters who used God's law of confession to overcome the world they lived in.

Shadrach, Meshach, and Abednego weren't the only Hebrew boys who had an experience with the Persian government. Daniel had enemies too, because he was the king's very favorite. So his enemies managed to pass a law stating that he couldn't pray to God. They knew he prayed several times a day.

> Then said these men, We shall not find any occasion against this Daniel, except we find it against him concerning the law of his God.
>
> Then these presidents and princes assembled together to the king, and said thus unto him, King Darius, live for ever.
>
> All the presidents of the kingdom, the governors, and the princes, the counsellors, and the captains, have consulted together to establish a royal statute, and to make a firm decree, that whosoever shall ask a petition of any God or man for thirty days, save of thee, O king, he shall be cast into the den of lions.
>
> Now, O king, establish the decree, and sign the writing, that it be not changed, according to the law of the Medes and Persians, which altereth not.
>
> Wherefore king Darius signed the writing and the decree.
>
> Daniel 6:5-9

Daniel refused to stop openly praying and worshipping God, so he was brought before the king. King Darius loved Daniel and was upset that he had signed such a stupid law, but he still had to keep it. Daniel had been such a powerful witness to the king, however, that it was the king who made the confession of faith that would save Daniel!

> Then the king commanded, and they brought Daniel, and cast him into the den of lions. Now the king spake and said unto Daniel, Thy God whom thou servest continually, he will deliver thee.
>
> Daniel 6:16

This king fasted and prayed for Daniel all night. The next morning he ran to the den of lions and was relieved to find Daniel alive and unharmed. The first thing he did was to have everyone who had conspired against Daniel—and their families—thrown into the lions' den, where they were all killed. Then he made the following decree:

> Then king Darius wrote unto all people, nations, and languages, that dwell in all the earth; Peace be multiplied unto you.
>
> I make a decree, That in every dominion of my kingdom men tremble and fear before the God of Daniel: for he is the living God, and stedfast for ever, and his kingdom that which shall not be destroyed, and his dominion shall be even unto the end.
>
> He delivereth and rescueth, and he worketh signs and wonders in heaven and in earth, who hath delivered Daniel from the power of the lions.
>
> Daniel 6:25-27

Darius went even further than Nebuchadnezzar in honoring God. Nebuchadnezzar had decreed no one could speak against God, but Darius commanded his people to fear God and know that He was the Most High. Daniel's faith turned an empire's heart toward God.

Joshua and Caleb changed the government of an entire region when they confessed they were able to take the land God had given them and then did exactly that. When they got there, the Canaanites still inhabited the Promised Land, and their government was determined to hold onto the land. But they couldn't hold it. They had to turn it over to the men who had confessed God's Word! So Joshua and Caleb took possession of it, just as they had said they would.

When they came into the Promised Land, Caleb said to Joshua,

> And now, behold, the LORD hath kept me alive, as he said, these forty and five years, even since the LORD spake this word unto Moses, while the children of Israel wandered in the wilderness: and now, lo, I am this day fourscore and five years old.
>
> As yet I am as strong this day as I was in the day that Moses sent me: as my strength was then, even so is my strength now, for war, both to go out, and to come in.
>
> Now therefore give me this mountain, whereof the LORD spake in that day; for thou heardest in that day how the Anakims were there, and that the cities were great and fenced: if so be the LORD will be with me, then I shall be able to drive them out, as the LORD said.
>
> Joshua 14:10-12

Caleb was a man of faith, and the Lord had to give him his inheritance. Although he was eighty-five years old, he had the strength to fight and take the part of the Promised

Land he believed God wanted him to have. He had the strength because he had exercised the law of confession for the last forty-five years. So he and Joshua overturned an old, entrenched government and brought the government of God into the Promised Land.

The Law of Confession Overcomes Nature

Nature's storms, earthquakes, and other disasters should never intimidate believers. Dealing with natural disasters, which the world often calls "acts of God," is part of our challenge in living on Earth today. But Jesus demonstrated how the law of confession overcomes nature. He got into a boat with the disciples on the Sea of Galilee and said they were going to cross to the other side. The Bible says that suddenly a freakish, clearly demonic storm arose, and it looked like the boat was going to sink. What was Jesus doing? Sleeping peacefully!

> And there arose a great storm of wind, and the waves beat into the ship, so that it was now full.
>
> And he was in the hinder part of the ship, asleep on a pillow: and they awake him, and say unto him, Master, carest thou not that we perish?
>
> And he arose, and rebuked the wind, and said unto the sea, Peace, be still. And the wind ceased, and there was a great calm.
>
> And he said unto them, Why are ye so fearful? how is it that ye have no faith?

And they feared exceedingly, and said one to another, What manner of man is this, that even the wind and the sea obey him?

Mark 4:37-41

Jesus expected the disciples to handle the storm by themselves, and they could have. Earlier in the same chapter He had taught them about the power of the Word of God being spoken. They were to confess it until it became revelation to them, then the Word would become their boat. The Word was holding them! They got to the other side because the Word never fails. There are no leaks in that boat!

Another good example of how the law of confession overcomes natural laws can be found in Luke, chapter 5. Jesus had borrowed Peter's boat to preach from, and to bless Peter in return He said in verse 4, "Launch out into the deep, and let down your nets for a draught," or a great catch. Peter and his partners had been fishing all night and had caught nothing. Now it was daylight, and the fish could see the net. It was not a good time to go fishing, but Peter did as Jesus directed and caught a net-breaking, boat-sinking load of fish.

Jesus overcame a natural law (the best time to catch fish is at night) with a greater spiritual law: the law of confession. He spoke the result He desired—a great catch. In case you're wondering, we know that what He spoke was also God's will. Jesus said He never did anything He didn't see the Father do (John 5:19). When Jesus said, "Let down your nets for a draught," He was saying what the Father was saying, and *homologeo* superseded natural law. Those fish had to jump right into that net.

It says in verse 9 that Peter and his partners were astonished at the number of fish they caught, but Jesus wasn't astonished one bit. Why? Because He understood the law of confession. He had said what God wanted to happen, He believed in His heart it would happen, and therefore He confidently expected a net-breaking catch of fish no matter what time of day it was.

If you get ahold of this truth, it will change your life forever. You'll stop looking at the natural things you always thought were holding you back. Whether it is a natural disaster or fish that aren't biting, you have God on your side. That is the deciding factor. You win because God is with you. Jesus stopped the storm and everyone marveled at His authority over nature. You have that same authority!

Again, the only thing that can keep you from fulfilling all God has called you to do, is you.

The Law of Confession Overcomes False Prophets

We have already quoted the verse of Scripture that says, " God is not a man that he should lie" (Numbers 23:19). It is interesting to see who said this and why they said it. In the Old Testament, Israel was about to attack Moab and take that part of the Promised Land that God had given them. The king of Moab, Balak, became afraid and hired a prophet named Balaam to curse Israel.

Balaam was a soothsayer (Joshua 13:22) who lived in Mesopotamia (Deuteronomy 23:4). People knew he was a prophet, but he did not serve God. He served himself. That is why he is called a false prophet (2 Peter 2:1-15) even though he prophesied correctly. God does not judge us by our performance but by our heart. Although Balaam's performance was true, his heart was evil.

Which [false prophets] have forsaken the right way, and are gone astray, following the way of Balaam the son of Bosor, who loved the wages of unrighteousness.

2 Peter 2:15 [brackets mine]

Woe unto them! for they have gone in the way of Cain, and ran greedily after the error of Balaam for reward, and perished in the gainsaying of Core.

Jude 1:11

But I have a few things against thee, because thou hast there them that hold the doctrine of Balaam, who taught Balac [Balak] to cast a stumblingblock before the children of Israel, to eat things sacrificed unto idols, and to commit fornication.

Revelation 2:14 [brackets mine]

Balaam prophesied for money, and he loved unrighteousness. He turned many people to sin (Numbers 31:16). When Balak asked Balaam to curse Israel and said he would pay him for it, of course Balaam agreed. But what is interesting is that he still acknowledged God as the Most High God. He went through all the rituals a prophet of Israel would go through to please God (Numbers 23:1-6), however, his motivation was only to get his own way—to curse Israel and get paid for it. In the end, God gave him this word to say:

> And he took up his parable, and said, Balak the king of Moab hath brought me from Aram, out of the mountains of the east, saying, Come, curse me Jacob, and come, defy Israel.
>
> How shall I curse, whom God hath not cursed? or how shall I defy, whom the LORD hath not defied?
>
> Numbers 23:7-8

Balak was furious and took Balaam to another place to curse Israel. Again, Balaam made the proper sacrifices and God gave him the following word to say:

> And he took up his parable, and said, Rise up, Balak, and hear; hearken unto me, thou son of Zippor:
>
> God is not a man, that he should lie; neither the son of man, that he should repent: hath he said, and shall he not do it? or hath he spoken, and shall he not make it good?
>
> Behold, I have received commandment to bless: and he hath blessed; and I cannot reverse it.
>
> Numbers 23:18-20

In the end, Balaam was killed by the army of Israel (Numbers 31:8). He is a terrifying example to all of us of someone who knew the sovereign power of God and yet lived according to his selfish lusts. He knew the truth but never surrendered his life to God and to His Word. Instead of serving God with His whole heart, he used the gift God gave him for his own personal gain. Still, because he acknowledged God he could not prophesy anything but what God said.

Now there are other prophets and people in the world who do not acknowledge God or His Word, and they do plenty of cursing. They curse God, they curse His people, and they do everything they can to pervert and distort His Word. A lot of these people utter curses and think they are doing good. For example, in some Eastern and New Age religions they have what they call "affirmation," which is saying what you want to happen. You could also call this a positive confession.

The difference between an affirmation or positive confession and a believer's confession of faith is clear and simple. An affirmation is what that person wants; our confession of faith is what God wants. A positive confession is that person's words; God's law of confession uses only His Word. God only performs His Word. He isn't backing anything else anybody says, no matter how positive or affirming it is.

Even Balaam knew that the law of confession changes the world, and he tried to get what he wanted through it. But God overrode his desire to curse Israel and caused him to bless Israel. God is not a man that he should lie, and the Word of God will stand forever. If an evil man like Balaam could prophesy so powerfully (and everything he prophesied came to pass because it was God's Word), then what can we as children of God be doing?

We should never be intimidated by the ignorant and evil declarations of false prophets because God's Word is always the last word. Regardless of what some guru said on television or what another pundit said in a magazine or newspaper, we can be confident that when we declare and decree God's Word, it will come to pass.

The Law of Confession Overcomes the Temporal Things of This World

For our light affliction, which is but for a moment, worketh for us a far more exceeding and eternal weight of glory;

While we look not at the things which are seen, but at the things which are not seen: for the things which are seen are temporal; but the things which are not seen are eternal.

2 Corinthians 4:17-18

To really understand the law of confession, you first have to grasp the idea that nothing in this world is permanent or certain. On the other hand, the Word of God stands forever. Temporal means subject to change, and that includes all the things you can physically see, hear, touch, taste, or smell. But the "things which are not seen" are eternal. These are the promises of God in His Word. They stand and prevail no matter what is going on in the world around you.

Paul gives us the key to living according to eternal truth instead of temporal circumstances: we aren't to focus on the things we see but focus instead on the things we cannot see. In other words, we are to keep our eyes on the Word. We are to see the world with spiritual eyes instead of just our natural eyes. God's Word is Spirit and life. His promises are the eternal things we need to be focusing on. Instead of looking at the situation, we should look at His promise because His promise is what is certain. Everything else is subject to change.

Maybe my natural eyes see a sickness. This is what the natural world is telling me. But I am to look at the promise in the Bible which says, "by His stripes ye were healed" (1 Peter 2:24). That is the eternal truth that will overcome the temporal situation I am dealing with. My total health and healing may not be seen in the natural, but I see it in the spirit—and the spirit realm overrides the natural realm.

When we acknowledge the supremacy of the eternal things of God over the temporal things of this world, we declare light in darkness. We demonstrate that the kingdom of darkness is expelled by the kingdom of light. In Genesis 1:2, God acknowledged that the Earth was covered in darkness, but that was all. From the moment He saw the problem, He began speaking the answer. In verse 3 He said, "Light be," and light was. He didn't talk about the darkness at all because He knew the darkness of this world was temporal, but the light of God was eternal.

Your faults and weaknesses are also temporal, but who you are in Jesus Christ is eternal.

For ye see your calling, brethren, how that not many wise men after the flesh, not many mighty, not many noble, are called:

But God hath chosen the foolish things of the world to confound the wise; and God hath chosen the weak things of the world to confound the things which are mighty;

And base things of the world, and things which are despised, hath God chosen, yea, and things which are not, to bring to nought things that are:

That no flesh should glory in his presence.

1 Corinthians 1:26-29

Your old carnal, earthly, worldly self cannot be right or do right. But when you were born again you became a new creature in Christ Jesus. All those sins, faults, and weaknesses passed away and you became brand new. Now you can do all things through Christ who strengthens you (Philippians 4:13). God knows you can't do it in your own strength, but He can and wants to do it through you.

Because God does all the work of strengthening and making you new, you aren't going to get any credit for it. This is what is meant when the Scripture says, "that no flesh should glory in his presence." The whole responsibility of manifesting what is eternal into this temporal world is His not yours. All He asks you to do is speak what He tells you to speak in faith. He wants you to function exactly the way He does. Don't comment on the problem, just thank Him and declare the solution—which you can only see with your spiritual eyes.

The only reason the devil still has any influence in the Earth is because the church has not received what God has promised us. God has given us the ability to speak those things that be not as though they were (Romans 4:17) and obtain all things that pertain to living a godly life (2 Peter 1:3), but we have not been bold to speak His Word and overcome everything the world does to stop His plan.

God needs a voice to overcome the world today, and we are His voice.

12

Be Fully Persuaded

Therefore it is of faith, that it might be by grace; to the end the promise might be sure to all the seed; not to that only which is of the law, but to that also which is of the faith of Abraham; who is the father of us all,

(As it is written, I have made thee a father of many nations,) before him whom he believed, even God, who quickeneth the dead, and calleth those things which be not as though they were.

Who against hope believed in hope, that he might become the father of many nations, according to that which was spoken, So shall thy seed be.

Romans 4:16-18

Abraham had no hope in what his natural eyes and the world offered him. He was too old to have children, and so was his wife Sarah. The world was against all hope, but Abraham hoped against that hope. He looked at that which was eternal, believed that promise of God, and spoke his new name again and again. "I am Abraham, the father of a multitude." He spoke what couldn't be seen with the natural eye or understood by the natural mind because what He said was spirit and life.

You can apply this to your life because Abraham is your father in the faith (verse 16). Maybe you have lost a great deal of money in a business deal or an investment that went bad. All the enemy wants you to do is say you're broke. He can work with that confession and make sure you stay broke. So don't look at your empty wallet or bank account. Look at the promises God made to you in His Word, promises that every part of your life will prosper as your soul prospers (3 John 1:2), and that He will supply all you need (Philippians 4:19).

Remember that natural circumstances are subject to God's eternal truth. His Word trumps all. Read in Matthew 14:15-21 about how Jesus fed the multitudes on five loaves and two little fish. Read in 1 Kings 17:10-16 how Elijah multiplied the little food the widow woman had during a terrible drought. Read in Matthew 17:27 about how the disciples needed money to pay tribute and Jesus told them to check a fish's mouth, or in Luke 5:1-6 when Jesus gave the disciples a miracle catch of fish. Then you will begin to have some Bible hope.

People may tell you, "Don't get your hopes up." Don't listen to them! Their idea of hope is not the biblical hope we have in God's promises. Get your biblical hope as high as you can and watch God get involved. Nothing is impossible for God when you believe Him and confess His Word. You are not confessing what the pastor told you to confess. You are not confessing what your brother or sister or spiritual mama or daddy told you to confess. You are confessing what God said. If He didn't say it and if you didn't hear Him say it in your heart and believe it, then it has no business coming out of your mouth. But if He said it and His words are alive in your heart, then shout it from the rooftops!

Don't Stagger

And being not weak in faith, he considered not his own body now dead, when he was about an hundred years old, neither yet the deadness of Sarah's womb:

He staggered not at the promise of God through unbelief; but was strong in faith, giving glory to God;

And being fully persuaded that, what he had promised, he was able also to perform.

Romans 4:19-21

Abraham didn't consider his own body because it was temporal and subject to change. He only considered the promise of God because it was eternal and certain. He didn't stagger around, going back and forth, looking at his old body during the day and looking at the stars in the sky during the night. No, he was consumed only with what God had said.

Staggering is what James called being double-minded, and that never works. The law of confession cannot work if you go back and forth between two beliefs.

But let him ask in faith, nothing wavering. For he that wavereth is like a wave of the sea driven with the wind and tossed.

For let not that man think that he shall receive any thing of the Lord.

A double minded man is unstable in all his ways.

James 1:6-8

Any instability in your life is due to not believing and speaking the Word of God. To live a stable life, you are going to have to consider only what God says, no matter how bad it looks and no matter how your flesh is screaming at you. You have to stay focused on the promise and stagger not. If you stay focused on His Word, you will not be double-minded. You will stick with your belief in God's Word and accept nothing less than what He says. And that means you will get what you say!

When I was flying fighter planes in the Air Force, I had a radar screen that showed me a picture of what was in front of me. I could adjust the sweep on that screen to reveal 25 miles out, 50 miles out, 100 miles out, and even 250 miles out. I would see blips on the screen for whatever was there. My job was to pick out and focus on my target. I would take a cursor, which worked like a mouse on a computer, and point it at the target I wanted to hit. Once I pressed that cursor, everything but that target disappeared from the screen.

In that natural analogy, if there was any other object on the screen that was a threat to me, I was vulnerable. I could only see my target. But in the spirit, when I am only seeing

God's promise to me, when that becomes my target, I am fully protected. God has my back! I can put my cursor (my heart) on that promise, press it (speak my confession of faith), and know that what God said has got to come to pass.

Abraham staggered not at the promise of God because he was fully persuaded that God was able also to perform it. That's another key right there. Who had promised? It was God who had promised, and it was God who was going to perform it. It wasn't up to Abraham to perform it, and it isn't up to you or me to perform it. What we have to do is believe God's promise, speak His promise, and let Him do the rest. He said He would, and He will. It's a law!

False Humility

To have the faith of Abraham, you have to believe that God is on your side. He is not only *able* to perform His Word, but more than anything He *wants* to perform His Word to bless you. This is true humility. You take God at His Word. So many believers miss it because they start saying, "I'm so unworthy. I've said and done so many terrible things." They need to stop that! They are contradicting the Word of God and giving the enemy the opportunity to condemn and depress them.

You are worthy of God's blessing because the blood of Jesus cleansed you from all sin—past, present, and future. You are not worthy because you had a perfect day and never had an evil thought. You are not worthy because you go to church, pay your tithes, and pray a lot. If you missed it yesterday and said something you regret, that doesn't make you unworthy either. You are worthy because God says you are worthy by the blood of the Lamb. Period.

When a born-again believer continues to speak this kind of low self-esteem, self-condemning talk, it dishonors God and what Jesus did for them on the Cross. It also says they don't believe what God says in His Word about them. He has given their spirit a new birth. He has filled them with His Spirit. He has made them His own child and given them His nature and authority. They are a joint-heir with King Jesus. That makes them royalty, and they have part ownership of everything Jesus has. So for them to say they are not worthy or blessed is dishonoring Him.

What I'm talking about here is false humility, and it has no place in the believer's heart, mind, or mouth. False humility is a total obsession with self. Think about it. You cannot beat up on yourself if your eyes are on Jesus, who brings God's unconditional love and forgiveness into your life. You can only beat up on yourself and talk about how awful you are if you are focusing on yourself and all your faults.

The key to walking in the Spirit is to focus on Jesus and take your eyes off yourself. Put self off your mind, and then you will stop criticizing and disqualifying yourself. If you are thinking about Jesus and all He has done and is doing for you, you won't be criticizing yourself. And if you do sin, 1 John 1:9 says all you have to do is repent and you are forgiven and cleansed. There is no reason to cry over spilt milk! Just get right, get free, and get going with the Lord again!

Abraham refused to look at himself or consider his body. He kept his eyes on the promise of God and meditated on all those stars in the sky that represented his descendants. He thought about how big and powerful God was and how much God loved him. He didn't think on anything other than the fact that God wanted to bless him in every way possible. That is true humility!

True humility is being humble and grateful that God loves you and values you beyond what you can think or imagine. False humility is being full of yourself—all your faults, failures, weaknesses, and sins. If you have a problem with false humility, you need to meditate day and night on what God says about you in His Word. You can't get arrogant about that because you will also see that you are nothing without Him! But you are everything in Him.

You are the righteousness of God. You are more than a conqueror. He always causes you to triumph in Christ. You are saved. You are delivered. You are healed. You are rich. You are full of wisdom. Even so, you don't have to fulfill the promise. God has said it and He will make it good. Your part is to humbly and boldly say what God has said and believe it in your heart.

Dealing With Unbelief

Because the law of confession hinges on belief, it's important that you understand a couple of related terms: non-belief and unbelief. There is no such thing as non-belief. Everyone believes something. An atheist believes there is no God, but that is still a belief. You cannot exist believing nothing because God created humans in His image, and He believes. Therefore, we believe—something.

Unbelief, on the other hand, is a God term. It is a biblical term that means you do not believe what God said. In simple terms, God says unbelief is not agreeing with Him and His Word. Unfortunately there has been a great deal of unbelief in the Church. You hear people say, "God's going to heal you," but that's not what God said. In 1 Peter 2:24, He said, "By His stripes ye were healed"—past tense. If you are waiting on God to heal you, you can forget about ever being healed. God says you have already been healed by the stripes Jesus bore on His back. He has healed you already, and saying what He says is believing.

There are also two kinds of believing—secular believing and Bible believing. Secular believing is based on experience and human reason. You believe something because you have experienced it or have reasoned it out. It makes sense to your natural mind and lines up with what your physical senses perceive. Secular believing will not get you the promises of God. On the other hand, Bible believing is based solely on the Word of God without any external evidence to support it. You believe it just because God said it.

This is not always an easy thing to do, especially when all hell has broken loose around you.

And one of the multitude answered and said, Master, I have brought unto thee my son, which hath a dumb spirit;

And wheresoever he taketh him, he teareth him: and he foameth, and gnasheth with his teeth, and pineth away:

and I spake to thy disciples that they should cast him out; and they could not.

He answereth him, and saith, O faithless generation, how long shall I be with you? how long shall I suffer you? bring him unto me.

And they brought him unto him: and when he saw him, straightway the spirit tare him; and he fell on the ground, and wallowed foaming.

Mark 9:17-20

In this account, a man brought his demon-possessed son to the disciples, but they could not cast the demon out. So the man brought his son to Jesus, and Jesus expressed some frustration saying the whole generation of people He was ministering to was filled with unbelief. He calls them a "faithless generation." He might have said, "Is there no one in this time who will believe God's promises?"

Then Jesus addressed the boy's father.

And he asked his father, How long is it ago since this came unto him? And he said, Of a child.

And ofttimes it hath cast him into the fire, and into the waters, to destroy him: but if thou canst do any thing, have compassion on us, and help us.

Jesus said unto him, If thou canst believe, all things are possible to him that believeth.

And straightway the father of the child cried out, and said with tears, Lord, I believe; help thou mine unbelief.

Mark 9:21-24

This was an honest father! He said he believed, but he had seen so much. The demon had ravaged his child for so many years that his faith was weak—but at least he recognized that fact.

What happened next indicates that Jesus must have had compassion on the man and honored the faith he did have.

> When Jesus saw that the people came running together, he rebuked the foul spirit, saying unto him, Thou dumb and deaf spirit, I charge thee, come out of him, and enter no more into him.
>
> And the spirit cried, and rent him sore, and came out of him: and he was as one dead; insomuch that many said, He is dead.
>
> But Jesus took him by the hand, and lifted him up; and he arose.
>
> Mark 9:25-27

All things are possible to those who believe God and His Word, so that father must have had enough belief to have his son set free. This illustrates that what is possible for me may not be possible for you. Maybe I can believe more than you can. What's possible for me is based solely on my capacity to believe what God says. If God tells me that a corporate jet is mine to help me minister His Word around the world and I believe it—don't be jealous of me when I get it! And don't look down on me if I'm still growing in believing in an area you have become fully persuaded about. That's why God set us in a body of believers; we are to help one another in our unbelief in the same way Jesus helped this boy's father.

Start where you are and develop your faith because developing faith erases unbelief. We all start out with the same "measure of faith" (Romans 12:3), which God gives each of us when we're born again. We can develop our faith by hearing and meditating on the Word. As it says in Romans 10:17, "So then faith cometh by hearing, and hearing by the word of God." We can also develop our faith and get rid of unbelief by praying and fasting, spending quality time with the Lord. This is what Jesus told His disciples when they asked Him why they couldn't cast out the demon.

> And when he was come into the house, his disciples asked him privately, Why could not we cast him out?
>
> And he said unto them, This kind can come forth by nothing, but by prayer and fasting.
>
> Mark 9:28-29

Many believers have been taught that some demons won't come out unless they pray and fast, but the real issue Jesus was dealing with here was the condition of the disciples' hearts. He was dealing with their unbelief. Their spirits had been overwhelmed and intimidated by the natural circumstances. They saw the demon break and tear the boy. The demonic show of strength seemed so great. Jesus said, "You need to fast and pray and grow in faith to the point where any physical manifestation will not move you. Only the Word of God will move you."

We need to get all unbelief out of our lives by praying and speaking and believing God's Word over and over. Like Abraham, who kept saying his new name over and over, we have to keep saying what we believe. Our faith grows strong and confident and bold as we hear the Word again and again. Then, when we are placed in a terrible situation, where only the miraculous power of God will help, we will be full of faith to meet the challenge.

> And Jesus answering saith unto them, Have faith in God.
>
> For verily I say unto you, That whosoever shall say unto this mountain, Be thou removed, and be thou cast into the sea; and shall not doubt in his heart, but shall believe that those things which he saith shall come to pass; he shall have whatsoever he saith.
>
> Mark 11:22-23

Many of us learned Mark 11:23 very early in our walk of faith. It is key to developing the faith God has given us, which will defeat any unbelief in us. Since speaking is mentioned three times and believing only once in that verse, that says to me that I'd better keep on saying His Word out loud or it won't make any difference what I believe. I have to do the speaking part consistently in order to receive the promise.

Notice something else about this verse. It doesn't say, "shall not doubt in his head." It says, "shall not doubt in his heart." You can't believe with your head. You have to believe with your heart, or your spirit. If you do, you shall have whatever you say. It's a law. God already has said "Yea" and "Amen" to every promise (2 Corinthians 1:20). There's never a "No" or a "Maybe so" with God. When you believe it in your heart and speak it with your mouth, you will have what you say.

Another thing to notice in Mark 11:23 is that it says, "those things" that you say will come to pass. You can't say foolish, negative things all day and then think the blessings you pray over yourself at night will come to pass. When you say things you don't really mean, you are building unbelief in your heart.

You are the prophet of your own life, and you must train your mouth to say only what you really believe and want. Abraham didn't conceive Isaac by complaining about his dead body during the day and then thanking God for His promise at night. He stayed the course. He never waivered from the promise.

> And this is the confidence that we have in him, that, if we ask any thing according to his will, he heareth us:
>
> And if we know that he hear us, whatsoever we ask, we know that we have the petitions that we desired of him.
>
> 1 John 5:14-15

Our confidence is the same confidence Abraham had: we are asking according to His will and therefore He hears us; and if He hears us, it is done. Remember, God doesn't hear anything but faith. His ears do not function on the frequency of doubt and unbelief. His ears only hear words that come out of believing hearts. So when our believing hearts speak, He hears and performs His Word. That's the law of confession.

When you speak God's Word in faith, believing, you know that you have the promise. If you ask in line with His Word and His will, you have it. If you know you have something, why would you pray for it again? Just praise Him and thank Him!

If you don't know that the promise of God is yours, then deal with your unbelief. Saturate yourself with God's Word and pray in the Spirit to build up your most holy faith (Jude 20) until you are fully persuaded He will perform His work in your life. Then pray with confidence, believing in your heart and confessing with your mouth what God has said. He wants to bless you just as much as He blessed Abraham.

13

Master Your Mouth

For in many things we offend all. If any man offend not in word, the same is a perfect man, and able also to bridle the whole body.

Behold, we put bits in the horses' mouths, that they may obey us; and we turn about their whole body.

Behold also the ships, which though they be so great, and are driven of fierce winds, yet are they turned about with a very small helm, whithersoever the governor listeth.

James 3:2-4

James had a lot to say about the tongue. He begins by saying that if we get to the point where we don't say one offensive word, we will be able to control our whole body. By controlling our tongue, we would not fulfill the lusts of our flesh. Our spirits, led by the Holy Spirit, would be ruling and reigning completely over our lives—all because we reached the point where we never said a word that didn't agree with God and His Word.

To "offend not in word" does not mean we would never offend another human being. We can tell people about Jesus and they can be offended. We can provoke a brother or sister to love and good works and they can be offended. What this means is that we would never utter a word that would offend God or go against His Word.

James goes on to compare the tongue to the bit in a horse's mouth. A rider holds onto reins, which are directly connected to a metal bar or bit in the horse's mouth. By pulling on the reins, the rider controls how and where the horse will go. If you have ever ridden a spirited horse, you know what a good illustration this is of how difficult it is to control the tongue! Just like a horse that wants to go its own way, it takes a lot of strength, patience, and perseverance to tame the tongue.

With the horse, you're putting pressure on his tongue to get him to do what you want. Likewise, if you want to change the circumstances in your life, you will have to apply some pressure on your tongue to bring your flesh in line because your flesh will not want to cooperate. Your tongue is used to saying whatever seems right to your natural mind. The Word doesn't make sense to your carnal thinking, which thinks it's right to "tell it like it is." But you are going to have to tell it like God and the real you want it to be.

James then compares our tongue to the rudder on a large ship. He says that ships are great and driven by fierce winds. Our senses and minds are constantly being bombarded by ungodly pictures and ideas in all forms of media, in our schools, at our place of work, and even on billboards as we drive to church. And there is always somebody crossing our path who may offend us, hurt us, or just ruin our day. We cannot escape these fierce winds that urge us to use our tongues to speak words that do not line up with God's Word. But we must accept that responsibility! We are that governor at the helm of our ship, turning that rudder (our tongue), and determining which direction we will go by the words that come out of our mouths.

The path or direction that a great ship takes is determined by a very small thing. The rudder, which is cutting through the water behind the ship, is connected to the helm or steering wheel up on deck. The captain turns the helm, which turns the rudder. At first, the rudder will just plow through resisting water; but if it's left in that position, in time it will cause the entire ship to turn and change direction. Just a slight change in the rudder eventually will cause a tremendous change in course for a large ship.

In the same way, when you first start confessing what the Word says about your situation, lining up your confession with the promise in the Word, your words may seem to be just plowing through the mess you are in. But if you keep on your course by holding fast to the confession of your faith, gradually your situation will begin to turn. It won't be long before you will be amazed at the difference.

Kindling the Fire

Even so the tongue is a little member, and boasteth great things. Behold, how great a matter a little fire kindleth!

James 3:5

James called the tongue a little member that could boast great things and start great fires in the hearts of people. The tongue is like kindling to a fire. When I was young, my parents would take my brother, my sister, and me down to Georgia to stay for awhile at my grandparents' farm. Sometimes we would visit around Christmas, and the weather would be pretty cool. My grandfather would get up early in the morning to heat the house.

My grandparents had a potbelly stove and a fireplace, so Granddad would first get some kindling. This is wood that usually has some sap on it—a syrupy substance easy to ignite. He would light the kindling and take it over to the stove or put it in the fireplace. Then he would put some large pieces of wood on top of it. The kindling would ignite the wood and we'd have a big fire in no time. Soon you couldn't see the kindling at all because the flames were so big.

James is explaining that your tongue works the same way that kindling does. Some words you said, or some words someone else said to you, might have started a fire that has raged in your life for years. But those words are like the kindling. You can't see the kindling once the fire is raging. You may not know what you said or what someone else said to you that set this fire off in your heart.

And the tongue is a fire, a world of iniquity: so is the tongue among our members, that it defileth the whole body, and setteth on fire the course of nature; and it is set on fire of hell.

For every kind of beasts, and of birds, and of serpents, and of things in the sea, is tamed, and hath been tamed of mankind:

But the tongue can no man tame; it is an unruly evil, full of deadly poison.

James 3:6-8

You don't know the root cause of what's destroying your life or making you miserable. It is like your life is always spinning out of control. Addiction. Hatred. Terror. Jealousy. Your flesh just can't get enough, and you feel like you're living in hell half the time. You can't find the source because that kindling is so small in comparison to the great fire of destruction it has caused. But God knows what it is! He wants to lead you back to where that kindling was lit, when those words were spoken and lit that fire. Then you can start saying something different and reverse the blaze that's burning in your life. Instead of a fire of self-destruction, you will have a peaceful and passionate fire for God burning in your heart.

You might say, "Well, Pastor Winston, a violent temper just runs in my family." But it can't just happen that way. Things like violent tempers or depression or promiscuity don't "just run." Nothing happens without words. You may not know who spoke the words and when, but words started it. Words are behind any kind of destruction that you see in your family line. But here's the good news: If words started it, words can stop it. You just have to put in the rudder and start turning the situation around.

Start by cursing those words of doubt and unbelief that you, and maybe others as well, spoke in the past. Render that bad seed dead by the cleansing blood of Jesus Christ and the delivering power of the Holy Ghost. Plead the blood of Jesus over that seed and decree that it will not harvest. Then start planting in your heart the new seed you've found in the Word. Begin speaking the truth over you, your family, and your situation.

What you have to do is get the Word so big in your heart that it dominates everything that comes out of your mouth by continuing to say what God says. When you say what God says repeatedly in faith, God's going to honor it. There is nothing on this Earth so great or powerful that it cannot be turned around with your tongue. Stop saying your problem runs in your family. Cut that off now! Your tongue is going to change the course your family has been on and move you from destruction to blessing. Your tongue will kindle a new, godly fire in your heart and spread quickly to every member of your family.

A Sweet Fountain

Therewith [with our tongue] bless we God, even the Father; and therewith [with our tongue] curse we men, which are made after the similitude of God.

Out of the same mouth proceedeth blessing and cursing. My brethren, these things ought not so to be.

Doth a fountain send forth at the same place sweet water and bitter?

Can the fig tree, my brethren, bear olive berries? either a vine, figs? so can no fountain both yield salt water and fresh.

James 3:9-12 [brackets mine]

What happens when you mix sweet water and bitter? You end up with bitter water. The bitter will contaminate the sweet. You can't keep them separate if they are coming out of the same fountain, and the one pollutes the other. If you talk all kinds of unbelief, going on and on about your circumstances and your problems, you can't just throw in a faith statement and expect it to work. Your spirit isn't going to believe it. There's just too much unbelief in there.

Proverbs 18:8 says, "The words of a talebearer are as wounds, and they go down into the innermost parts of the belly." Words are so much more than sound. They are spirit, and they can go all the way down into your spirit and stay there. That can happen when somebody speaks a hateful word or a condemning word. The person it was spoken to can remember that word, and it will kindle a fire of self-loathing within them for years. People rehearse these words. They can still hear these words being spoken and it affects their lives.

Telling a child, "You won't ever amount to anything. You're gonna be just like your daddy," and then the next minute saying, "You are God's child and anything is possible with God," is not going to produce a confident child of faith. The first statements of unbelief and deception pollute and distort the truth of the second statement. This is a fountain that is contaminated by unbelief because the tongue has not been tamed.

No matter how a child is acting, don't speak anything to them that doesn't line up with the Bible. "You're not smart enough" is not edifying and it should never come out of your mouth. I don't care what the grades are or what the teacher says. If that child wants to be a doctor, then encourage that child and help that child to become what God has put in their heart. Tame your tongue! Release only fresh, clean water. Put out those old fires of discouragement and defeat that were started long ago.

James 3:8 says that no person can tame the tongue. But Jesus can! In fact, He always has His tongue under the control of the Spirit. He did when He walked this Earth, He does now, and we can do all things through Him (Philippians 4:13). By ourselves we cannot live godly lives, but with Him we can bring forth all the fruit of the Spirit and change our lives (John 15:5).

You might be looking at the shape your life is in right now and be totally downcast. It just seems hopeless. It is like your past has made your present a very dark place to be in. By yourself, that's the way things will stay. But with God's help, you can change what you say and speak light to your life. Just like your Father God spoke "Light be" to the dead, dark Earth, He will help you speak His Word into your life and work all things for your good (Romans 8:28). In Him, you can become a sweet fountain whose waters bring life and produce great fruit for everyone you meet.

Wisdom From Above

Who is a wise man and endued with knowledge among you? let him shew out of a good conversation his works with meekness of wisdom.

But if ye have bitter envying and strife in your hearts, glory not, and lie not against the truth.

This wisdom descendeth not from above, but is earthly, sensual, devilish.

For where envying and strife is, there is confusion and every evil work.

But the wisdom that is from above is first pure, then peaceable, gentle, and easy to be intreated, full of mercy and good fruits, without partiality, and without hypocrisy.

And the fruit of righteousness is sown in peace of them that make peace.

James 3:13-18

When I read this passage of Scripture, the first thing I think about is those television shows that do nothing but sow envy, strife, and confusion. The host will march someone out who has been very mistreated and then shock them by bringing out the very person that used them and abused them. What they are doing can never bring forgiveness, healing, and restoration. All this does is produce more evil work. It feeds the flesh not the spirit.

The wisdom of this world is earthly, sensual, and demonically inspired. It says that the more you talk about your problems, the better you will feel. People on talk shows will say things like, "I was abused when I was twelve."

"How old are you now?"

"I'm sixty years old."

"And you still haven't gotten over that?"

"No, I never will. Everyday I feel the same pain I felt all those years ago, like it just happened."

What happened was terrible and it captured their heart. Now, out of the abundance of their heart they are speaking—and the cycle of self-destruction goes on and on. That person must be born again. Only Jesus and His Word are powerful enough to get that poison out of their heart and out of their mouth. In Him they can purge their conscience of all the death and destruction in their past. They can uproot that evil tree that's been growing in their heart all these years.

It doesn't matter how a person was physically or sexually abused, humiliated in school, or lied to as a child. Whatever they are dealing with began because the wrong words were spoken. Even if their molester never said anything, their actions spoke volumes. "You're no good. This would never happen to a good girl." Whether the words came from a person or were whispered in their ear by a demon, those words went deep into their spirit and produced envy, strife, confusion, and every evil work.

Then one day they are promised that if they'll tell about it on a television show, if they'll just talk it all out, they'll be better off. Instead, when they start talking about it their bitterness spills out and spreads to the audience. The people in the audience start getting mad at someone they don't even know. Don't watch those kinds of programs! All they do is cause people to rehearse their hurts and stir up the flesh. That's the devil's trick, and he loves that kind of thing because it keeps people in bondage to him.

> There is a way which seemeth right unto a man, but the end thereof are the ways of death.
>
> Proverbs 14:12

Worldly wisdom says, "Talk about it. Get it out. Rehearse it. The more you talk about it the better you will feel." But God's wisdom says you will have what you say. When you keep talking about your problem, you just reinforce it and make it bigger. You put it deeper into your spirit, into your heart. To change your life, you have to stop talking about the problem and begin speaking the answer. Speak God's words of truth to bring His abundant life into your life. That's how you break free of the pain of your past and enter a bright, new future.

> Then said Jesus to those Jews which believed on him, If ye continue in my word, then are ye my disciples indeed;
>
> And ye shall know the truth, and the truth shall make you free.
>
> John 8:31-32

We are going for absolute, complete freedom. That means we must live absolutely and completely in the Word of God. Sometimes it isn't a huge problem like an addiction or sexual abuse that we are dealing with, it might be something as simple as forgiving someone. Our tongue needs to be forgiving.

Staying mad at someone and talking to all your friends about them might feel good to your flesh, but it will block your prayers. Jesus talked about that in Matthew 5:23-24. He said (my paraphrase) "Don't come to the Father with your prayer requests if you and someone else have offended one another. Get things right with that person before you come to God for help." That is the wisdom from above. The wisdom from above is "pure, then peaceable, gentle, and easy to be intreated, full of mercy and good fruits, without partiality, and without hypocrisy" (James 3:17).

God's wisdom will always bring peace. James 3:18 said that the proof of our righteousness in Christ Jesus is that we sow words of peace and make peace wherever we go. If our words stir up trouble, we are probably not acting out of the wisdom and righteousness of God. We are acting out of worldly wisdom.

The Holiness Factor

Follow peace with all men, and holiness, without which no man shall see the Lord.

Hebrews 12:14

Speaking the positive things the Word says about us is necessary, but we have to be careful where we go with it. Some believers get ahold of the law of confession and the life-changing power of taming their tongue and it becomes works to them. They read scriptures like Hebrews 12:14, which says we are to pursue holiness in order to see the Lord, and they start trying to act holy by speaking holy. The problem is, they already are holy through Jesus! They just need to act out of His holiness.

Too many believers also think they have to be what they consider holy in order to receive from God. The devil can trip us up when we decide that holiness is in what we say and do. Again, we are already holy because of the blood of Jesus. He has made us holy in Him. I didn't quite understand this just after I got saved, and as a result I let the devil steal my car.

When I got saved, I owned a Corvette. It was a great car for me at the time, but I thought that a humble, holy Christian should not be driving a Corvette around town. So I put it up for sale at a ridiculously low price because I also didn't think truly holy believers should have much money. When my ad hit the newspaper, I was flooded with calls. One man was coming all the way from Gary, Indiana, to Chicago to buy it from me, but I sold it to the first guy who came around with cash.

Later, the fellow from Gary told me, "Mister, you gave that car away." I realized then that he was right. I had been blinded by religious nonsense. I had not been led by the Word of God. Holiness is not in how much money you have or what you drive. You can be holy on a Harley! Holiness is not where you live, how you dress, or even what you say. Holiness is who you are in Him. When you understand this, then what you say will flow from the reality of holiness within you. It's not a hard thing! It's the way God created us to be: to speak and live out of the abundance of our hearts which are holy in Him.

You can't make taming your tongue about works. The Word says in James 3:8 that no human being can tame their tongue. You can't do this in your natural wisdom and strength. You can only tame your tongue and change your life by saying what flows from that place of peace and holiness in your spirit. This place of peace within, where the Holy Spirit lives, is where you have all the wisdom and power you need to tame that little member and move the mountains in your life.

Against All Fear

Throughout the Bible, God tells us again and again not to be afraid.

> After these things the word of the LORD came unto Abram in a vision, saying, Fear not, Abram: I am thy shield, and thy exceeding great reward.
>
> Genesis 15:1

> ...Be strong and of a good courage; be not afraid, neither be thou dismayed: for the LORD thy God is with thee whithersoever thou goest.
>
> Joshua 1:9

> For I the LORD thy God will hold thy right hand, saying unto thee, Fear not; I will help thee.
>
> Isaiah 41:13

But when Jesus heard it, he answered him, saying, Fear not: believe only, and she shall be made whole.

Luke 8:50

And when I saw him, I fell at his feet as dead. And he laid his right hand upon me, saying unto me, Fear not; I am the first and the last:

Revelation 1:17

These are just a few of the many verses of Scripture that tell us we are not to be afraid, that God is always with us— protecting us, providing for us, and keeping us well and whole. But fear is one of the storms of life that all of us battle from time to time, and some of us battle it daily. The law of confession is our answer. We can either continue to speak words of fear and make it worse, or we can decide to do what Jesus did in Mark 4:39. We can stand up and command that storm of fear to go, declaring, "Peace! Be still."

Nothing but words can stop a storm. Jesus was a Word man, this is a Word planet, and when Jesus ministered He continually said, "It is written." He never did anything that wasn't in the Word. When He commanded the storm and said, "Peace, be still," He was speaking what the Scripture said in Psalm 89:9: "Thou rulest the raging of the sea; when the waves thereof arise, thou stillest them." He knew that God's Word overcomes anything we face in the natural world.

If it's not written in or doesn't line up with God's Word, all our commanding and declaring is not going to make it happen. But when we speak the Word that has been written, there is no limit to what can be done. We can stop enemy missiles, cancer, a bad attitude, and every kind of fear, worry, anxiety, and terror we face in our world today. Words are more powerful than anything Satan can devise to scare us.

E. V. Hill's Story

There was a preacher named E. V. Hill, who grew up very poor in Texas during the Depression. One of the major reasons he succeeded was that his mother understood the power of the law of confession. In an era when most black families in the South could not afford to send their children to school, she was determined that E. V., who was her oldest boy, would get an education. The deacons at her church kept telling her he was a big boy and should be helping her in the field and with the younger children, but Mrs. Hill would not hear of that. She would say again and again, "My boy is going to school."

E. V. graduated from the eighth grade in a one-room schoolhouse, first in his class. (He always mentioned that he was the *only* one in his class!) He went on to high school and again graduated first (and only) in his class. Then he was accepted at Prairie View A&M University. September finally came, and it was time for him to go to college.

Mama wrapped his cardboard suitcases with twine to hold them together and gave E. V. a paper bag with some fish sandwiches. They were so oily, he had to hold the bottom of the bag to keep them from falling out. Before he boarded the bus, Mama gave him all the money she had—

$17.95. She said, "Son, this is all Mama got, but I'll be praying for you."

When E. V. got to school he signed up for his courses, but then he had to pay for them. He only had about five dollars left, and the school didn't take credit cards in those days, even if he'd had one. But he got in the cashier's line just as if he had the money to pay his bill. The devil was telling him in one ear, "Get out of line, you fool. You are making a fool of yourself." In the other ear, he heard Mama saying, "I'll be praying for you. My son is going to school."

E. V. chose not to be afraid but to trust God, because he knew it was God's will for him to be in school. He kept moving up in line and the devil kept taunting him, trying to bring doubt and unbelief. E. V. kept putting down those doubts, resisting the devil, and believing God instead. When he was one person away from the cashier's cage, a big man he had never seen came up to him and said, "Excuse me, are you Hill?"

He answered, "Well Sir, my Mama said...."

But the man interrupted him and asked again, "Are you E. V. Hill?" He nodded. "Get out of line."

E. V.'s head dropped, and he fought the fear that he was about to be sent home. He followed the man to a corner of the room and watched as he opened up a portfolio. Then he said, "Hill, I don't know what's happening here, but I've got a four-year scholarship for you. Got all your books paid for and a monthly stipend." He wasn't supposed to be in line because God had already taken care of everything!

Because of his mama's confession that her son was going to school, money came. And her son became one of the most respected preachers and Christian leaders of our time. No one who knew or heard E. V. Hill will ever forget him because he understood the power of speaking God's Word and will. You couldn't be around him without hearing something that would change your life. He was a man who learned early on how to overcome fear by standing on God's Word and keeping your faith confession.

Overcoming fear is one of the Church's biggest opportunities to reveal the saving, healing, and delivering power of Jesus in these last days. But too often we've been taught that the storm is bigger than we are, instead of that God is bigger than the storm. We haven't been taught that when we speak His Word, God gets involved and that settles it. The truth is, if we just believe God's Word and speak it, He is obligated to carry it out because He has put His Word above His name and must abide by His law of confession.

When the Unexpected Comes

We can prepare ourselves for tomorrow every way we know how, but then one day something happens that we never could have anticipated. We are only human, and the Bible says in 1 Corinthians 13:12 that we see darkly—we miss things and don't see everything that's ahead. The devil also knows this and tries to take advantage of our blind spots whenever he can. When a crisis happens that we didn't expect, that's when we have to watch what we say more than ever.

There's a powerful illustration of this in the story of Jacob and his wife Rachel, which you can read in Genesis 28-31. Jacob wanted to marry Rachel and had agreed to work seven years for her father, Laban, in order to get her. At the end of the seven years, Laban slipped his older daughter Leah in Jacob's tent on the wedding night instead. Jacob was furious, but he agreed to work seven more years to get Rachel.

At the end of the seven years, Laban gave Rachel to Jacob, but through the years he had also cheated Jacob by changing his wages. The blessing that Jacob had been given by his father, Isaac, was coming on Laban because Jacob was working for him. Laban was growing rich, while Jacob was doing all the work and getting nowhere. Jacob just couldn't get ahead.

Finally, Jacob got a plan from the Lord to outsmart his deceiver. He received the knowledge he needed from God and proposed a deal Laban couldn't refuse. This deal made Jacob rich at Laban's expense, because Jacob was living by faith and believing God to do what He had promised. It wasn't long before Jacob became so prosperous that Laban and his sons were becoming more and more hostile toward him. Jacob knew it was time to take his family and his goods and move away from his father-in-law.

Jacob did not trust Laban, so he left without telling him. As soon as Laban figured out that his son-in-law and two daughters and everything they owned were gone, Laban went after them. But he didn't go after them just because he wanted to say good-bye or even to try to take some of

Jacob's things. Someone had stolen his religious idols and Laban wanted them back.

Jacob didn't know that his beloved wife, Rachel, had stolen her father's household idols and had hidden them among her baggage. When Laban caught up with Jacob, He asked him why he had left without letting him say good-bye to his daughters. Jacob said, "Because I was afraid: for I said, Peradventure thou wouldest take by force thy daughters from me" (Genesis 31:31). So we see that Jacob was in a state of fear at this point. Then this is what he had to say about the idols:

> With whomsoever thou findest thy gods, let him not live: before our brethren discern thou what is thine with me, and take it to thee. For Jacob knew not that Rachel had stolen them.
>
> Genesis 31:32

Jacob gave Laban permission to search every camel and tent for his idols, and when Laban got to Rachel's tent she sat upon them and told him she had searched her tent and had not found them. When the idols failed to turn up, Jacob thought Laban was lying again; but of course, he wasn't this time.

In a time of fear and being anxious about Laban coming after him, his wives, his children, and his wealth, Jacob was hit with the unexpected: the stealing of Laban's idols, which was a serious offense. Without praying or finding out all the facts first, he rashly declared that whoever took Laban's idols would not live. He had pronounced the death of his own wife without realizing it. He believed that every word he spoke would come to pass, and it did. When Rachel gave birth to Benjamin, she died in childbirth.

It is true that Rachel should not have taken the idols. She was trying to bring her old pagan ways into her new life with the God of Abraham, Isaac, and Jacob her husband. Like Lot's wife who looked back longingly to Sodom as it was being destroyed and turned into a pillar of salt (Genesis 19:26), Rachel should have known that the Most High God does not mix with other gods. Still, she might have repented and lived had Jacob never spoken death over her.

This story is a good one to remember when something sneaks up behind us and catches us by surprise. That is the time to be quiet! We should never speak from our fear. We should always speak from our faith. When fear strikes, we need to seek God and His Word before we open our mouths to say anything. Once we have His will and Word on the situation, no matter how we feel, then we can declare it in faith and turn that situation around.

It's Not About Emotion

Sometimes when something is frightening us, we will get God's will and Word on it and peace will just flood our whole being. We can speak the Word with full assurance that He will perform what He has promised. But other times we may get God's will and Word about our problem and our emotions just won't settle down for some reason. Deep inside we know the truth and believe the truth. Our spirit is in a state of peace. But on the outside our emotions are still riding high on fear.

The law of confession works on faith in God's Word, not on emotion. Your flesh can be shaking, but when you believe and speak the Word you know in your heart it is done. On the other hand, you can get up and yell and cry for an hour and never get anywhere with God because it is all just an emotional release. God is not looking at emotion, nor is He looking for emotion; He is listening for faith in His Word. Remember, He only hears His Word spoken in faith.

This is good news when you cannot seem to calm your emotions. You still "feel" fearful, even though you know that God's Word is true and will overcome the situation. When this happens, just speak the Word in faith. This is what the Bible calls courage. Courage is speaking the Word in faith no matter how you "feel" or what is going on in your carnal mind and emotions.

Before God told Joshua not to fear, he told him three times to be strong and of a good courage (Joshua 1:6-9). He knew that sometimes the emotion of fear lingers even when we know the truth and begin speaking the truth. But I will also tell you this from personal experience: the more you speak God's Word in faith, the more that emotion of fear loses its power over you. Eventually, the supernatural peace in your spirit will flow into your soul and body and that fear will be thrown out.

God does not want you to fear. You must take this seriously, because He does.

He that overcometh shall inherit all things; and I will be his God, and he shall be my son.

But the *fearful*, and unbelieving, and the abominable, and murderers, and whoremongers, and sorcerers, and idolaters, and all liars, *shall have their part in the lake which burneth with fire and brimstone: which is the second death.*

Revelation 21:7-8 (italics mine)

The subject is overcoming, and the Greek word translated "fearful" is *deilos*. It means "timid, fearful," and some synonyms would be "fainthearted, with a small soul, little spirited."[1] We are not talking about the emotion of fear but the condition of the soul and spirit. This word is not describing the emotion of feeling frightened. This word describes a spirit that is weak and a soul that is not transformed by the Word of God. This person is timid, which means they have no faith in God or His Word. Their only response to anything frightening is to run and hide because they have no Word in them.

Notice Revelation 21:8 follows "fearful" with "and unbelieving." That's because fear and unbelief go together. Do you see why fear is your enemy? Do you understand why God tells you again and again not to fear? It is because He hates unbelief, and unbelief is the basis for all kinds of fear, from the slightest tension to the darkest terror. Only believing God's Word will cure you of fear.

People are fearful and lack courage because they do not believe God or His Word. All the rest of the sins listed follow when we do not believe God's Word. We do not lack courage because we *feel* frightened. We lack courage when we don't choose to believe God, confess His Word, and do what He has called us to do—no matter how we feel.

David Overcame Fear

Even most unbelievers in the world know the story of David and Goliath. People love this story because we can all identify with the little guy who goes up against a giant. We love it when that little guy wins! Many of our movies follow this same theme—courageously the underdog defeats the big, strong opponent—whether it is in the boxing ring or on the battlefield. Our hearts thrill when the one no one expected to last the first few minutes gets the victory in the end. David is the prototype for all these heroes.

> And the Philistines stood on a mountain on the one side, and Israel stood on a mountain on the other side: and there was a valley between them.
>
> And there went out a champion out of the camp of the Philistines, named Goliath, of Gath, whose height was six cubits and a span.
>
> And he had an helmet of brass upon his head, and he was armed with a coat of mail; and the weight of the coat was five thousand shekels of brass.
>
> And he had greaves of brass upon his legs, and a target of brass between his shoulders.
>
> And the staff of his spear was like a weaver's beam; and his spear's head weighed six hundred shekels of iron: and one bearing a shield went before him.
>
> 1 Samuel 17:3-7

Goliath was a giant, and his weapons and his armor were bigger and more powerful than anything anyone in Israel had ever seen. This guy was scary! But it wasn't just how he looked. It was also what he said.

> And he stood and cried unto the armies of Israel, and said unto them, Why are ye come out to set your battle in array? am not I a Philistine, and ye servants to Saul? choose you a man for you, and let him come down to me.
>
> If he be able to fight with me, and to kill me, then will we be your servants: but if I prevail against him, and kill him, then shall ye be our servants, and serve us.
>
> And the Philistine said, I defy the armies of Israel this day; give me a man, that we may fight together.
>
> 1 Samuel 17:8-10

Goliath said that all he wanted was to fight one man, and whoever won that fight would determine who won the war between Israel and the Philistines. The whole army of Israel froze in fear because they were completely overwhelmed by the size, strength, and boldness of the giant. Then little David showed up. His father had sent him to bring food to his older brothers and to see how they were doing. David did not react the same way everyone else did when he heard Goliath rant and rave about destroying Israel.

> And David spake to the men that stood by him, saying, What shall be done to the man that killeth this Philistine, and taketh away the reproach from Israel? for who is this uncircumcised Philistine, that he should defy the armies of the living God?
>
> And the people answered him after this manner, saying, So shall it be done to the man that killeth him.

And Eliab his eldest brother heard when he spake unto the
men; and Eliab's anger was kindled against David, and he
said, Why camest thou down hither? and with whom hast
thou left those few sheep in the wilderness? I know thy
pride, and the naughtiness of thine heart; for thou art
come down that thou mightest see the battle.

And David said, What have I now done? Is there not a cause?

1 Samuel 17:26-29

Notice what happened when David spoke words of faith
and not fear. His older brother Eliab jumped all over him!
That's what can happen when everyone around you is
walking in fear and you come in walking in faith. Either
they will love you for bringing them to their senses and
reminding them that God is bigger than their problem, or
they will hate you for exposing and challenging their fear.
They'll accuse you of not facing facts and dealing with
reality. But the truth is, when you live by the Word of God
you deal with true reality: facts will change when God's
truth is applied!

When it was clear that David would fight the giant, King
Saul asked to see him. He told David he was too young to
fight the giant.

And David said unto Saul, Thy servant kept his father's
sheep, and there came a lion, and a bear, and took a lamb
out of the flock:

And I went out after him, and smote him, and delivered it
out of his mouth: and when he arose against me, I caught
him by his beard, and smote him, and slew him.

Thy servant slew both the lion and the bear: and this uncircumcised Philistine shall be as one of them, seeing he hath defied the armies of the living God.

David said moreover, The LORD that delivered me out of the paw of the lion, and out of the paw of the bear, he will deliver me out of the hand of this Philistine.

1 Samuel 17:34-37

That was enough for Saul. He tried to get David to wear his armor, but David turned him down. The armor was too big and not suitable. You have to know what works, and David knew what worked. He didn't know Ephesians 6:16, but he had a shield of faith that was sufficient to quench every fiery dart of the enemy. And Goliath was throwing a lot of those at him.

And when the Philistine looked about, and saw David, he disdained him: for he was but a youth, and ruddy, and of a fair countenance.

And the Philistine said unto David, Am I a dog, that thou comest to me with staves? And the Philistine cursed David by his gods.

And the Philistine said to David, Come to me, and I will give thy flesh unto the fowls of the air, and to the beasts of the field.

1 Samuel 17:42-44

David stood there with his only weapon, a sling and five smooth stones, and listened to this huge warrior insult him and his God. If there was any fear in David, it was replaced with a righteous anger that anyone would speak against the God who had delivered him from the lion and the bear.

Then said David to the Philistine, Thou comest to me with a sword, and with a spear, and with a shield: but I come to thee in the name of the LORD of hosts, the God of the armies of Israel, whom thou hast defied.

This day will the LORD deliver thee into mine hand; and I will smite thee, and take thine head from thee; and I will give the carcases of the host of the Philistines this day unto the fowls of the air, and to the wild beasts of the earth; that all the earth may know that there is a God in Israel.

And all this assembly shall know that the LORD saveth not with sword and spear: for the battle is the LORD's, and he will give you into our hands.

1 Samuel 17:45-47

David used the law of confession to defeat any fear of his own, his nation's fear, and the forces of evil they were fighting. When David turned down Saul's offer of armor for the fight, he knew he had something better: a covenant with Almighty God. Notice he didn't state his deliverance in terms of the future. He said, "This day." You don't need to stay with a problem for long when you attack it with the words that come from the abundance of God's Word in your heart.

First Peter 4:11 says, "If any man speak, let him speak as the oracles of God." David knew it wasn't up to him to defeat Goliath. When he spoke the oracles of God, God would do it. He knew God could stop a whole army with one man's mouth, and He did. He didn't know exactly how God was going to do it, and He didn't put God in a box or limit how he could do it. David just confessed his faith and then acted in faith. He did what he had peace to do.

And it came to pass, when the Philistine arose, and came, and drew nigh to meet David, that David hastened, and ran toward the army to meet the Philistine.

And David put his hand in his bag, and took thence a stone, and slang it, and smote the Philistine in his forehead, that the stone sunk into his forehead; and he fell upon his face to the earth.

So David prevailed over the Philistine with a sling and with a stone, and smote the Philistine, and slew him; but there was no sword in the hand of David.

Therefore David ran, and stood upon the Philistine, and took his sword, and drew it out of the sheath thereof, and slew him, and cut off his head therewith. And when the Philistines saw their champion was dead, they fled.

1 Samuel 17:48-51

Later David wrote in Psalm 27:1, "The Lord is my light and my salvation; whom shall I fear? the Lord is the strength of my life; of whom shall I be afraid?" He was probably remembering the time he ran toward his enemy, shouting what he believed. That's the way we need to face our fears. If we are afraid because someone has called us a name and said terrible things about us, we can answer with the Word of God: "In the name of Jesus I reverse that curse. No weapon formed against me shall prosper. I am righteous, holy, and God's beloved through the blood of Jesus Christ."

Whether your enemy is a giant of disease, a giant of financial lack, a giant of family problems, or a giant of temptation to sin—the law of confession can defeat it and bring you into that place of blessing. The Lord wants to share what belongs to Him with you, which is why He made you His joint-heir. He's given you authority in His name. He's told you that you can do whatever He did when He walked the Earth, and that you are to imitate Him in everything.

> Therefore be imitators of God [copy Him and follow His example], as well-beloved children [imitate their father].
>
> Ephesians 5:1 AMP

God likes it when you copy Him and act like Jesus. That's what He wants you to do. He put His own Spirit inside you, and He loves it when you let Him show up and show out!

Stop looking at your situation and thinking *you* have to solve it. All you have to do is speak God's will and Word to it. God won't do that part for you, so don't ask Him to! In Mark 11:23-24, Jesus told you to move the mountain of fear with your words of faith.

15

Waiting on Your Words

I ended the last chapter by saying that it wasn't scriptural for you to ask God to move your mountain. Jesus said in Mark 11:23-24, it was up to you to speak God's Word in faith and move that mountain with your words. The Bible says that it isn't by might or power but by the Spirit of God that mountains are moved (Zechariah 4:6). But the Spirit of God is waiting for you to speak, just like He waited for God to say, "Light be" before He released light to dispel the darkness that covered the Earth.

> And the earth was without form, and void; and darkness was upon the face of the deep. And the Spirit of God moved upon the face of the waters.
>
> And God said, Let there be light: and there was light.
>
> Genesis 1:2-3

The Spirit of God hovered over the problem of darkness. He was waiting for God to speak the Word. The moment God spoke, the Holy Spirit turned on the light. Today the Holy Spirit is still waiting for one thing: to hear the Word of God declared in faith. This time He is waiting to hear it spoken by the saints of God, so He can continue to bring God's love and light and power to the people of the Earth.

One Will Do

When I was in a foreign country, they were having elections and the incumbent running for re-election was a Christian. As a matter of fact, they had posted his baptism in water on the Internet. The other person who was running was of another religion, and there was a Christian bishop who kept saying that the Christian man would be re-elected. Other preachers were angry with the bishop because the opposing candidate had promised them some things for their vote, and so they were supporting the unbeliever. The Christian leaders had a big meeting and got into an argument about the political situation, but that bishop refused to back down.

The bishop kept confessing that the Christian president would be re-elected, and he received some death threats as a result, but God protected him. Finally the day of the election came, and the votes started pouring in. It looked pretty bad for the Christian gentleman through most of the day, but in the last hours, votes for him began to pour in. The next thing they knew, he moved out ahead of the opposition and was elected again.

That bishop's confession not only changed his life; it changed the life and direction of a nation. If they had elected someone who did not hear or follow Jesus, the nation would have been worse off. It's interesting that the bishop was almost standing alone in this battle, but the Word of God says, "there is no restraint to the Lord to save by many or by few" (1 Samuel 14:6). God can use one man or woman to change a nation. He waited for someone to speak His will in faith, and that bishop came along. His confession released God's power to bring the victory to that Christian gentleman and all the Christians of that nation.

God used Gideon—one man—to deliver Israel in the Old Testament. They were hiding from their enemies, and Gideon was no exception! God sent an angel to shake him up and give him his marching orders.

> And the angel of the LORD appeared unto him, and said unto him, The LORD is with thee, thou mighty man of valour.
>
> And Gideon said unto him, Oh my Lord, if the LORD be with us, why then is all this befallen us? and where be all his miracles which our fathers told us of, saying, Did not the LORD bring us up from Egypt? but now the LORD hath forsaken us, and delivered us into the hands of the Midianites.
>
> Judges 6:12-13

Notice the angel called Gideon, "Thou mighty man of valour," while he was hiding like a coward. That angel was calling things that be not as though they are! But angels can only say what God tells them to say. They cannot go against His Word. God saw what Gideon was to become and called him that. God has called you something too. He's called you more than a conqueror (Romans 8:37)!

Unfortunately, Gideon didn't get it. He was still too frightened and complained that the Lord had forsaken Israel to her enemies (the blame game again). He forgot all God's promises never to leave or forsake him. But the Lord pressed in on him.

> And the LORD looked upon him, and said, Go in this thy might, and thou shalt save Israel from the hand of the Midianites: have not I sent thee?
>
> And he said unto him, Oh my Lord, wherewith shall I save Israel? behold, my family is poor in Manasseh, and I am the least in my father's house.
>
> And the LORD said unto him, Surely I will be with thee, and thou shalt smite the Midianites as one man.
>
> Judges 6:14-16

The word of the Lord to Gideon was that he would "smite the Midianites as one man." When Gideon finally agreed, the Lord said something interesting to him.

> And the LORD said unto Gideon, The people that are with thee are too many for me to give the Midianites into their hands, lest Israel vaunt themselves against me, saying, Mine own hand hath saved me.
>
> Judges 7:2

To keep the Israelites from rising up in pride, convinced they defeated the Midianites in their own strength and numbers, the Lord had Gideon eliminate more and more of their numbers until there were only three hundred left.

Then they were totally outnumbered. In the natural it looked like there was no way they could win. And that was just how the Lord wanted it!

Human beings are always talking about numbers, their own achievements, and getting the credit. With God it is never about how many or how much, and it is always about Him getting the credit. He wants to get all the glory and keep us humble so we won't destroy ourselves through pride. So He gives us something beyond what our flesh can do, because then we will show forth His glory. Numbers 14:21 says, "All the earth shall be filled with the glory of the Lord," and it's going to come out of us! That's why He always puts us in impossible situations.

Gideon found himself in an impossible situation, and what did he do? He spoke the word of the Lord to his small army.

Arise; for the LORD hath delivered into your hand the host of Midian.

Judges 7:15

That army was so tight and in such agreement with the word of the Lord that they conquered the Midianites—just as Gideon has prophesied. Again, one man who spoke the Word of the Lord changed a nation.

Who's In Control?

If I asked you, "Do you believe God is in control?" you would probably say yes. It is true that God has ultimate and final control, but for the age we are living in, He gave dominion, which is control, over the Earth to mankind. He told Adam and Eve, "You run the place." At the time He gave them dominion, they were one with Him and they just naturally brought His presence and power wherever they went. They spoke from the abundance of their hearts, which knew nothing but God's will and Word.

After the Fall, Adam and Eve were spiritually separated from God. They spoke from the abundance of their hearts, and what did they say?

> And they heard the voice of the LORD God walking in the garden in the cool of the day: and Adam and his wife hid themselves from the presence of the LORD God amongst the trees of the garden.
>
> And the LORD God called unto Adam, and said unto him, Where art thou?
>
> And he said, I heard thy voice in the garden, and I was afraid, because I was naked; and I hid myself.
>
> And he said, Who told thee that thou wast naked? Hast thou eaten of the tree, whereof I commanded thee that thou shouldest not eat?
>
> And the man said, The woman whom thou gavest to be with me, she gave me of the tree, and I did eat.
>
> And the LORD God said unto the woman, What is this that thou hast done? And the woman said, The serpent beguiled me, and I did eat.
>
> Genesis 3:8-13

What a change! First they hid from God. Then the first thing out of Adam's mouth was that his excuse for hiding was that he was naked. It was all about him. When God, who knows everything, tried to get Adam to confess his sin, Adam blamed it on God for giving him the woman and then blamed the woman for giving him the forbidden fruit. God didn't get anything better out of Eve, who then blamed her actions on the serpent. No personal responsibility. No repentance. Just selfish self-centeredness and the blame game. This is what God had to work with from then on! How was He ever going to get His Word and will spoken into the Earth again?

Immediately God began to prophesy what He had planned from the foundation of the world: a second Adam would come and provide a way back to oneness with Him. From that moment on and through the generations, He chose someone to prophesy His plan—to speak it into the Earth—and write His Word so that the whole human race could know exactly what His plan was. It was a plan for complete redemption.

Finally, Jesus came just as the prophets had spoken.

> God, who at sundry times and in divers manners spake in time past unto the fathers by the prophets,
>
> Hath in these last days spoken unto us by his Son, whom he hath appointed heir of all things, by whom also he made the worlds;
>
> Who being the brightness of his glory, and the express image of his person, and upholding all things by the word of his power, when he had by himself purged our sins, sat down on the right hand of the Majesty on high.
>
> Hebrews 1:1-3

God's entire plan—the gospel—is summed up in the first three verses of the book of Hebrews. Jesus was God's mouthpiece for the last days, and we are joint-heirs with Him. That makes us His mouthpiece for the last days also.

Jesus made us righteous and restored us to oneness with Him. Jesus gave us all authority in His name. And before He ascended, He gave us the Great Commission.

> And he said unto them, Go ye into all the world, and preach the gospel to every creature.
>
> He that believeth and is baptized shall be saved; but he that believeth not shall be damned.
>
> And these signs shall follow them that believe; In my name shall they cast out devils; they shall speak with new tongues;
>
> They shall take up serpents; and if they drink any deadly thing, it shall not hurt them; they shall lay hands on the sick, and they shall recover.
>
> Mark 16:15-18

You are God's mouthpiece. It is up to you to release God's presence and power into this Earth just like all the prophets and Jesus did before you—with your words. The Holy Spirit is waiting and wanting to move, but if you never believe Him and speak His Word, He can't do anything. Your voice gives Him permission to do what God has wanted to do all this time: bless you, protect you, provide for you, and use you to bless, protect, and provide for others.

Do you see now that where the law of confession is concerned, you are in control? The Holy Spirit is in you, waiting to hear the Word of God come out of your mouth. That's the key—you have to believe that. Otherwise, you are just stumbling around on this planet, trying to make it to Heaven one day.

Bringing Heaven to Earth

Jesus didn't preach much about going to Heaven. He preached about Heaven coming to Earth. He said that was God's will. If God has been running everything on Earth why aren't we living Heaven on Earth? If He's in control, He's got everything in a mess!

The average church person would say that God is in control of everything, but He's not in control. Human beings are in control and are the ones who have made the mess. Now, believers have the responsibility to bring Heaven to Earth and we do that by doing what Jesus told us to do: preach the gospel and make disciples of all nations.

The gospel is the Good News and it is for all people. It is the only thing that will transform a person's life by restoring them to God and bringing them out of darkness into His marvelous light. Before He ascended, Jesus told us to go to the uttermost parts of the Earth and preach the gospel. This was how we were going to bring Heaven to Earth. Can Jesus go by Himself? No. He put His Spirit in His church and commanded us to go.

> For I am not ashamed of the gospel of Christ: for it is the power of God unto salvation to every one that believeth; to the Jew first, and also to the Greek.
>
> Romans 1:16

God's power is released when *we* preach the gospel. God and the angels do not preach or teach the Word. The angel came to a Gentile named Cornelius because he had been fasting, praying, and giving alms in order to get God to send someone who would preach the gospel to him. The angel said, "Cornelius, God has heard your prayer. Send a runner down to Joppa and tell this man named Simon Peter to come back here and preach to you." (See Acts 10:1-8.)

Why didn't the angel preach? Because he couldn't—he's not a human being! He has no dominion on the Earth. Sometimes we put down our flesh, but it is our physical bodies that connect us to the Earth and give us dominion over it. And although we are all looking forward to Heaven, while we are in our fleshly bodies we are to bring Heaven to Earth through the power of the gospel. That's exactly what Peter did when he went to Cornelius' house. Let's read what happened as he preached.

> While Peter yet spake these words, the Holy Ghost fell on all them which heard the word.
>
> And they of the circumcision which believed were astonished, as many as came with Peter, because that on the Gentiles also was poured out the gift of the Holy Ghost.
>
> For they heard them speak with tongues, and magnify God. Then answered Peter,
>
> Can any man forbid water, that these should not be baptized, which have received the Holy Ghost as well as we?
>
> And he commanded them to be baptized in the name of the Lord. Then prayed they him to tarry certain days.
>
> Acts 10:44-48

The Holy Ghost was just waiting for Peter to speak the Word of God so He could fall on those Gentiles, save them, and fill them. The Jews were astonished when the Spirit was poured out on Gentiles and they began speaking in tongues and magnifying God. Revival broke out in Cornelius' house and Peter stayed for "certain days" afterward to teach these new believers more of the Word of God.

Peter brought Heaven to Earth, specifically to the house of Cornelius. He understood that God was in charge of saving people and filling them with His Spirit, but He expected Peter to act in faith according to His Word. He knew from watching Jesus that everything that happened on the Earth had to be spoken by a human being, and if God's will was to be done, then a believer had to speak God's Word.

This idea that God's sovereignty rules everything in the affairs of people on Earth has really hurt the Church's ability to impact this world—and has given God the blame for a lot of things He had nothing to do with! For example in the last century, America's Church, believing God was in charge and not them, gave many of their country's institutions over to the enemy because they did not know or they did not practice the law of confession. They did not understand that they were the ones in authority, that their words would determine their future.

I believe if the law of confession had been taught in churches in the last century in America, Bibles and prayer would not have been taken out of our schools. Christians would have stepped up, boldly declaring God's Word, taking authority over the powers of deception and confronting the ungodly with their foolish thinking. But most believers didn't know the law of confession or operate in it, and they just turned the other cheek—which was out of context in that confrontation. As a result, the Church lost this major battle to the enemy and our public schools today are experiencing crime, perversion, and chaos our parents and grandparents couldn't even have imagined.

We can turn situations like this around by having total faith in the integrity and the power of our words spoken in agreement with God's Word. We are the generation that God is counting on to recover what earlier generations have lost. He wants us to go for the glory! But we must believe that when we decree and declare His Word, it shall come to pass, no matter who or what comes against us. Only a strong Church that understands the power of their words can reverse the ungodly trends in the institutions of their countries.

Heaven Right Now

On a more personal level, God does not want you to have even one bad day. Jesus has paid the price, and God has ordained the path that you should follow to receive the very finest He has. He wants you to have it. It can be yours if you believe it and speak it. He wants your life on Earth to be just like it is in Heaven.

When you practice the laws of the kingdom of God, like the law of confession, you are operating on His level of wisdom and knowledge—revelation knowledge. The wisdom you receive "from above" (James 3:17) will take you to greater understanding, blessing, and prosperity in every area of your life.

If you believe a promise of God, it becomes possible for you. And it shouldn't be that hard. You will believe an advertisement that may be the biggest lie ever told because you see it in the newspaper. It says that an appliance store is putting washing machines on sale in the morning for $99 when the doors open. Why don't you believe what you see in God's Word that easily?

People see a weather report saying that a hurricane is coming in two days, and masses of people will go out and buy lumber and start boarding up their houses. I'm not saying you should ignore those warnings, but how often are the weather reports wrong? Natural reports and information are constantly subject to change, but the Word of God stands forever. Yet Christians will believe the doctor who says they're sick but not the Word that says they're healed.

> If any of you lack wisdom, let him ask of God, that giveth
> to all men liberally, and upbraideth not; and it shall be
> given him.
>
> James 1:5

If you don't see how to move the mountain, ask! God created everything in this Earth, so He knows how it works. He wants to share His wisdom with you because then your faith will be greater and your ability to speak His will more effective. If you lack wisdom concerning how the devil got into your life or how he's keeping you from your prosperity, God wants to give it to you.

God won't call you a dummy and ask why you can't see the answer to your question. He will show you if it was something you said or did that is holding you back. Maybe someone agreed with you as well, and now it's come to pass. That's why it's in your life now. Then God will tell you what you have to speak to pull up that bad tree and get the right seed planted into your heart.

God has your life planned from beginning to end. He knows what you're capable of doing and He knows what you're going to need, next week and five years from now. He has it laid up in Heaven for you, but you have to cooperate with Him and do things His way. Every promise in the Bible has been put there for your benefit. You have to find your promise in the Word, speak it, believe it, and do whatever is necessary to act on it. Then it will surely come to pass.

The Word Works!

If believers get gut-level honest with me, they will tell me that their greatest fear is that the Word won't work after they speak it. They hesitate about speaking it and believing it. Of course, that makes them double-minded, and we know that a double-minded person can't receive anything from God. They won't receive because God could not hear what they said. He only hears words of faith.

There is something called mental assent, where you say you believe but do not really believe in your heart because your mouth says something entirely different. Here is an example of mental assent.

"Sister, do you believe the Word of God?"

"Oh yes, Sir."

"Do you believe all of it?"

"From Genesis to Revelation."

"All right. Praise God! Are you sick?"

"Yeah."

This dear sister just confessed that she is sick, but the Word of God says that she is healed. She gave mental assent to 1 Peter 2:24, but never got it planted deep in her heart, watered it with more scriptures on healing, and got to the point where she was fully persuaded. A person who practices mental assent stays on the level of the mind and never gets the Word down into their spirit. It is in their head intellectually, but it is not in their heart as reality. Thus they say they agree with the Word, but there is no fruit on their lips or in their lives.

You can say the Word is power, but has that seed ever been planted in your heart? When the deal goes down, are you trusting God and His Word or do you look to your own or someone else's thinking and abilities? I'm just waking you up because mental assent is big in the Church. That's what the enemy uses to keep you from really believing the Word works. He keeps you in fear that it won't work because you haven't been fully persuaded. The Word isn't deeply planted and growing in your heart.

For the word of God is quick, and powerful, and sharper than any twoedged sword, piercing even to the dividing asunder of soul and spirit, and of the joints and marrow, and is a discerner of the thoughts and intents of the heart.

Hebrews 4:12

Quick could also be translated "alive." The Word of God is first *alive,* and anything that is alive has purpose built into it because God created everything to have purpose. It is also powerful and sharper than a two-edged sword. Do you believe that? If you don't, I pray, and you should pray, for the eyes of your understanding to be enlightened. This is what Paul prayed for the saints at Ephesus.

Wherefore I also, after I heard of your faith in the Lord Jesus, and love unto all the saints,

Cease not to give thanks for you, making mention of you in my prayers;

That the God of our Lord Jesus Christ, the Father of glory, may give unto you the spirit of wisdom and revelation in the knowledge of him:

The eyes of your understanding being enlightened; that ye may know what is the hope of his calling, and what the riches of the glory of his inheritance in the saints,

And what is the exceeding greatness of his power to usward who believe, according to the working of his mighty power,

Which he wrought in Christ, when he raised him from the dead, and set him at his own right hand in the heavenly places.

Ephesians 1:15-20

Your eyes need to be opened to the spiritual power in the resurrection of Jesus. He confessed, "I'm going to Jerusalem. I'm going to be crucified, and I'm going to die. Three days later, I will come back to life." He confessed it. He believed it. And it happened exactly that way. While Jesus was dead, could anyone see the Word working? No! In fact, no one thought it was working. But it was!

> And he said, So is the kingdom of God, as if a man should cast seed into the ground;
> And should sleep, and rise night and day, and the seed should spring and grow up, he knoweth not how.
>
> Mark 4:26-27

We don't know how the Word does what it does. We don't know how the Holy Spirit turns water into wine, raises the dead, or parts the sea. But we don't have to know how. All we have to do is believe the truth: the Word works!

The Word will restore your soul!

The Word will bring your family out of strife and into peace and joy!

The Word will heal your body!

The Word will deliver you from all evil, sin, and temptation!

The Word will prosper your business!

The Word will give you wisdom to do an excellent job!

Believing God is simple. Just choose to believe it! But it seems when we come to the things of God, everybody takes on some kind of religious attitude that gets them all tied in knots and puts all the responsibility on them and their level of holiness. That is why it doesn't work because all they see is themselves, all they hear is themselves, and all they value is their own ability.

What I just described was spiritual death. There is no faith in God or His Word happening there. Everything is based on human thinking and ability. If that is you, then this is your answer: See Jesus, hear Him speaking the Word to you, then speak what He speaks and do what you see Him doing to express your faith in Him and His Word.

Speak the Word and let it do what God created it to do. Once you believe it and speak it, go do something else. Take care of your momma. Go to the bank and deposit that check. Meet your friend at your favorite restaurant. Play with your kids. Do your work in peace, knowing that the Word is working on your behalf—and it will not fail!

You can't make that Word come to pass any more than you can make that seed come up out of the ground. So you better just believe it, speak it, and rest. The Holy Spirit knows what to do!

Going Public with Your Confession

Some of us still are trying to hide our Christianity from the world, and it is time to take our confession public. This is a Word planet, and more than ever God needs voices speaking His Word and will in these last days. The Holy Spirit is hovering over the darkness of this Earth, waiting to hear us speak the Word.

In the past we have not been convinced that what we said was going to come to pass, and that has caused us to hold back or to abort what God was trying to do. But when we speak God's Word and will in faith from our hearts, what we say has to work every time. Jesus was certain whatever He said would come to pass, and He is our example.

When you begin decreeing a thing, it may not be immediately visible in the natural, but it will never become visible if you don't continue to believe what you say. The Word of God you speak is not a lie or deception. It isn't the world's idea of magic. It is putting the spiritual law of confession into operation—you will have what you say. It's taking the Word of God public.

You can't be timid and you can't care what people think about you when someone has a heart attack at work. That person's body can be healed and their life changed by the Word of God you believe in your heart and speak with your mouth. The lives of everyone who witnesses the miracle of the heart-attack victim's recovery will be changed. You speak God's Word and the Word will do what it does—bring Heaven to Earth.

Words are the only power and weapon that we have. God gave us the sword of the Spirit to be fruitful and multiply and take dominion. Our words can change and rearrange anything. The Lord described the power of His Word this way in Jeremiah 23:29: "Is not my word like as a fire? saith the LORD; and like a hammer that breaketh the rock in pieces?" Our words can create good or shatter evil.

Our generation has the awesome privilege to fulfill God's plan by replenishing the Earth with more disciples of the Lord, by restoring and extending the Garden of Eden throughout the world. We are to talk dominion and to take it. Because Adam dishonored the creative responsibility God had given him, we have been given the opportunity to succeed where he failed in doing the will of God.

When the universal Church recognizes the power of the law of confession and begins to speak with one voice, we will accomplish in God's way what the people of Babel were doing in a devilish way. We can bring Heaven to Earth. As we realize the full potential of God's plan for each of our lives and for this world, we will begin to see His kingdom coming and His will being done "on Earth as it is in Heaven."

ENDNOTES

Introduction

1 Noah Webster, *American Dictionary of the English Language,* 1828, (San Francisco, CA: Foundation for American Christian Education, 1967), "law."

2 *Ibid.*

2 The Confession That Brings Success

1 James Strong, *Exhaustive Concordance of the Bible,* "Greek Dictionary of the New Testament," (Nashville, TN: Thomas Nelson Publishers, 1984), #3670, #3674, #3056.

2 http://www.studylight.org/lex/grk/view.cgi?number=3670

3 Spiros Zodhiates, *The Complete Word Study Dictionary: New Testament,* (Chattanooga, TN: AMG Publishers, 1992), #3671.

4 Say What You Believe—Not What You Fear

1 James Strong, *Exhaustive Concordance of the Bible,* "Greek Dictionary of the New Testament," #3056, #4550.

5 When Pressure Comes...Just Say No!

1 Spiros Zodhiates, *The Complete Word Study Dictionary: New Testament,* #4567.

7 Made in His Image

1 James Strong, *Exhaustive Concordance of the Bible,* "Greek Dictionary of the New Testament," #4983, #4984, #4985.

2 *Ibid.,* #3402.

3 James Strong, *Exhaustive Concordance of the Bible,* "Hebrew and Chaldee Dictionary," (Nashville, TN: Thomas Nelson Publishers, 1984), #4390.

4 *Ibid.,* #85.

⁵ *Ibid.,* #8297, #8269.

⁶ Spiros Zodhiates, *Hebrew-Greek Key Word Study Bible* "Lexical Aids to the Old Testament" (Chattanooga, TN: AMG Publishers, 1984, 1991), #8282.

10 Believing the Best

¹ Spiros Zodhiates, *Hebrew-Greek Key Word Study Bible* "Lexical Aids to the New Testament" (Chattanooga, TN: AMG Publishers, 1984, 1991), #4982, #4991.

14 Against All Fear

¹ Spiros Zodhiates, *The Complete Word Study Dictionary: New Testament,* #1169.

PRAYER FOR SALVATION

Heavenly Father, You said in Your Word that whosoever shall call upon the name of the Lord shall be saved, so I am calling on Jesus right now. Lord Jesus, I believe You died on the Cross for my sins, and that You were raised from the dead. I ask You to come into my heart. Take control of my life and help me be what You want me to be. I repent of my sins and surrender myself totally and completely to You. I accept You and confess You as my Lord and Savior. Thank You, Father, for forgiving me, adopting me as Your child, and making me a new person. In Jesus' name I pray, amen.

Welcome to God's family!

If you prayed this prayer to receive Jesus Christ as your Savior for the first time, please contact us on the Web at **www.bwm.org** to receive a free book.

Or you may write to us at
Bill Winston Ministries • P.O. Box 947 • Oak Park, IL 60303

PRAYER FOR THE BAPTISM IN THE HOLY SPIRIT

My Heavenly Father, I am Your child, for I believe in my heart that Jesus has been raised from the dead and I have confessed Him as my Lord. Jesus said, "How much more shall your heavenly Father give the Holy Spirit to those who ask Him." I ask You now in the name of Jesus to fill me with the Holy Spirit. From this moment I confess that I am a Spirit-filled Christian. As I yield my vocal organs, in the name of Jesus I expect to speak in tongues for the Spirit gives me utterance. Praise the Lord! Amen.

Scripture References

John 14:16-17	Acts 2:4
Acts 19:2, 5-6	Ephesians 6:18
Luke 11:13	Acts 2:32-33,39
1 Corinthians 14:2-15	Jude 1:20
Acts 1:8	Acts 8:12-17
1 Corinthians 14:18,27	Acts 10:44-46

ABOUT THE AUTHOR

Bill Winston is a visionary leader whose mission is to empower believers through teaching and preaching the uncompromised Word of God, and to fulfill their highest calling and change the world through Jesus Christ.

Bill Winston received his Honorary Doctorate of Humane Letters from Friends International Christian University, and is Founder and Pastor of Living Word Christian Center, an 18,000-member church located in Forest Park, Illinois, and Tuskegee Christian Center in Tuskegee, Alabama. The church has a broad range of entities including the Joseph Business School (which includes a campus and on-line business school); Living Word School of Ministry and Missions; the Forest Park Plaza (a 32-acre shopping mall) and Washington Plaza (a shopping center in Tuskegee); Living Word Christian Academy; and many others. He also hosts the *Believer's Walk of Faith* television and radio broadcast, which reaches more than 200 million households nationwide and overseas.

Pastor Winston is also the Founder and Chairman of The Joseph Center® for Business Development, Chairman of the Board of Covenant Bank, President of New Covenant Community Development Corporation, Founder of Bill Winston Ministries (a ministry outreach that shares the Gospel through television, radio, and other media), and President and Founder of Faith Ministries Alliance (FMA), an alliance of more than 350 churches and ministries under the covering of Pastor Winston in the U.S. and overseas.

Pastor Winston is married to Veronica and is the father of three children, Melody, Nicole, and David.

To contact Bill Winston Ministries,
Please write or call

P.O. Box 947 • Oak Park, IL 60303 • 708-697-5100

Or visit him on the Web at
www.bwm.org

Please include your prayer requests
and comments when you write.

TRANSFORM YOUR THINKING, TRANSFORM YOUR LIFE

As you begin to change the way you think about yourself on the inside, the life of God begins to show up on the outside—your relationships, your finances, your career, even your health. Let the transformation begin and start to change your life from the inside out!

Dr. Bill Winston will help you discover the transforming power of renewing your mind. It may sound too simple that changing your thoughts could affect your entire life, but it is a scriptural truth threaded throughout the Bible and proven over thousands of years. Dr. Winston reveals that by focusing on who you are in Christ and the positive things God says about you in His Word, that Word will take a higher place in your mind than your current negative situations. You will discover the inner strength you need to overcome adversity and build success in every area.

Learn scriptural strategies that will get you out of the comfort zone of mediocrity, to help you think constructively and optimistically about yourself and your future to move you into the seemingly impossible, and develop the courage to achieve great things for God!

Regardless of your current circumstances, God has an abundant life for you. If you are not where you want to be, build a new way of thinking and see the transformation begin.

Now in Paperback!
Transform Your Thinking,
Transform Your Life
978-1-57794-971-8

THE KINGDOM OF GOD IN YOU

If the Kingdom of God is in us, why aren't we living lives of greatness in our world?

There are two kingdoms at work in this world, and tragically, even within the church, the majority of people are still living under the destructive lies and patterns of Satan's rule.

Dr. Bill Winston helps believers to start walking out their faith in miraculous ways. Why? We have a power within us that is supernatural and flies in the face of the world's arrogant—but ultimately inadequate—self-reliance on human understanding and effort.

With the faith of a child, even as small as a mustard seed, we unleash God's provision and power in our lives not by focusing on what we want, but by asking what the King of the Kingdom, God Almighty, wants us to accomplish. We quickly discover that our "grand" dreams and aspirations are miniscule in light of the greatness He has in store for us.

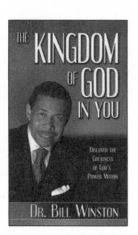

The Kingdom of God in You
978-1-57794-796-7

The Kingdom of God in You
Unabridged Audio Book
5 CDs
978-1-57794-997-8

The Kingdom of God in You
Digital Download for iTunes
978-1-57794-990-9

Available at bookstores everywhere
or visit **www.harrisonhouse.com**.

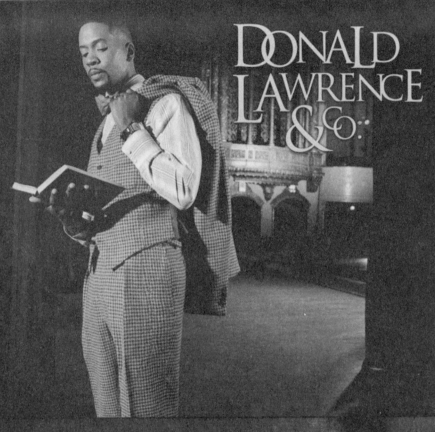

THE LAW OF CONFESSION, PART I

(INSPIRED BY THE TEACHINGS OF PASTOR BILL WINSTON)

THE BRAND NEW RELEASE FROM
GRAMMY AWARD WINNER & STELLAR AWARD WINNER
DONALD LAWRENCE

THIS LIFE-CHANGING RELEASE INCLUDES:
'THE BLESSING IS ON YOU,' 'LET THE WORD DO THE WORK,'
'THERE IS A KING IN YOU'
& THE INFECTIOUS LEAD SINGLE,
"BACK II EDEN"

IN STORES & ONLINE NOW!

Fast. Easy. Convenient.

For the latest Harrison House product information and author news, look no further than your computer. All the details on our powerful, life-changing products are just a click away. New releases, E-mail subscriptions, testimonies, monthly specials—find it all in one place. Visit harrison-house.com today!

harrisonhouse